IT'S A *Wonderful* Christmas

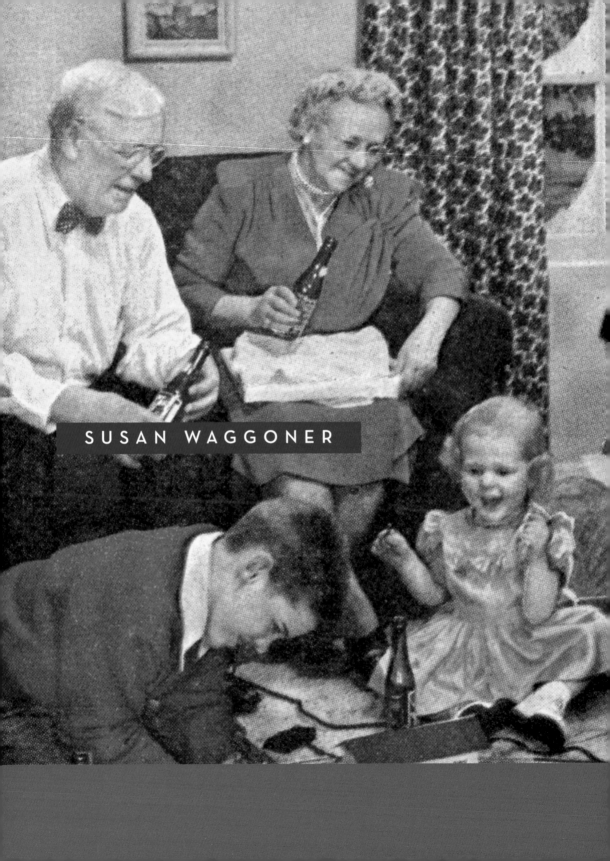

SUSAN WAGGONER

IT'S A *Wonderful Christmas*

THE BEST OF THE HOLIDAYS 1940–1965

S T E W A R T ,   T A B O R I   &   C H A N G
NEW YORK

Published in 2004 by
Stewart, Tabori & Chang
115 West 18th Street
New York, NY 10011

Canadian Distribution:
Canadian Manda Group
One Atlantic Avenue, Suite 105
Toronto, Ontario M6K 3E7
Canada

Cataloging-in-Publication Data
is on file with the Library of Congress
ISBN 1-58479-327-9

Designer: Kay Schuckhart/Blond on Pond

Production Manager: Jane Searle

The text of this book was composed in Adobe Caslon.

Printed in Singapore

10 9 8 7 6 5 4 3 2 1

First Printing

Stewart, Tabori & Chang is a subsidiary of

LA MARTINIÈRE
GROUPE

Contents

Tree and Trimmings

Throughout much of the world, for the past two millennia, Christmas has been the biggest event on the holiday calender. Yet Christmas has not always been the same from era to era. It has been celebrated in many different ways, shifting in focus and intent over the centuries. In colonial America, complaints about drunkenness and relaxed morals were common, but by the early 19th century, it had become more subdued and private, with most families celebrating quietly at home. Then came the Victorian era, a watershed replete with sentimental longings, a rising middle class, and a thrilling new array of manufactured goods. Those who like to decry the so-called "commercialization" of Christmas must look back more than a century — to all the porcelain dolls, painted tin soldiers, and lavishly decorated trees — to find the source of all the fuss.

Ironically, those consumer-oriented Christmases seem quaint by today's standards. Because, like other countries and other eras, 20th century America also left its stamp on Christmas. Not surprisingly, the biggest consumer society the world has ever known has made Christmas a bigger, brighter event than ever before, introducing colored electric lights, brightly colored wrapping paper and ribbons, new songs and stories, and a host of newly-minted traditions. Even during the depths of the Depression, Christmas was as lavish as people could possibly afford to make it. World War II added a layer of bittersweet poignance, with songs like "White Christmas" and "I'll Be Home For Christmas" expressing a deep longing for home and family. As soon as peace and prosperity returned, that dream was fulfilled. Families seemed determined to make up for lost time — to enjoy more, spend more, give more, and entertain more. The big American Christmas had been born. And, like so many Christmases before it, it all started with a tree.

THE TREE

Picture it — daughters raised on Laura Ingles Wilder and *Little Women* demanding old-fashioned trees festooned with tinsel squaring off against moms yearning for flocked trees in the latest, strictly modern color palette. Quite the donnybrook, and it was waged in millions of homes throughout the 1950s and 1960s. If only someone had told them that the traditional tree wasn't all that traditional, or pointed out that artificial trees date back father than anyone imagined.

For one thing, the Ingleses and Marches may have had Christmas trees — at least in the movie and TV versions — but few of their neighbors did. In 1900, only one in five American families had a tree. It took another 20 years for the custom to become truly commonplace. As for those towering European trees that figured in so many songs and stories, they were more or less for the wealthy. Centuries of cutting timber for firewood had vastly depleted Europe's forests, making lumber in any form expensive. Middle-class Europeans who wanted a "real" tree usually settled for table-top sizes, while poorer families made do with small artificial trees made of raffia, goose feathers, or other materials. Although lumber was never as scarce in America as in Europe, the time and expense of retrieving wood from the wild was significant, and artificial trees were available from the 1880s on. The first Christmas tree farms, which opened in the early 20th century to service large urban areas like New York, undoubtedly did much to make real trees available to all.

Like Americans, the British had been slow to adopt the German custom of putting up a tree, and only embraced it after Queen Victoria sanctioned the practice in the mid-1800s. When a wave of nostalgia for all things Dickensian swept America and Britain in the 1930s, the tree became a popular symbol of that lost era. Interest surged again after World War II, when Britons seeking the comfort of the past demanded trees in record numbers. Unfortunately, there were even fewer evergreens in England than in continental Europe, and many families could not afford the tree of their dreams. Rescue came from an unlikely source — the Addis Brush company of America. A manufacturer of toilet bowl brushes, Addis began making artificial brush tress in the 1930s. Over the next decade, thousands of Addis trees were sold in Britain.

Americans remained relatively uninterested in artificial trees so long as they attempted to imitate real evergreens. Then, in 1950, a turning point came. Addis patented a tree that made no attempt to resemble a freshly cut evergreen. The Silver Pine was

made of aluminum and came with a flood light and revolving color wheel that bathed the tree in different shades. In keeping with the streamlined tastes of the times, and the fact that putting electrical lights on a metal tree posed a safety hazard, no further decorations were really needed. The ultramodern tree had been born, and Americans quickly embraced it. Britons were a bit slower, preferring Addis's green brush tree until the 1960s, by which time the Americans were off to something else.

The fad of the 1960s was the flocked tree. Suddenly, through the miracle of chemisty, people could have a lush, thick tree coated with snow in any color imaginable. The country was awash in trees of gold, white, pink, pale blue, lilac, and — for the *very* sophisticated — black. Gone were the multicolored trees of old, decorated in mismatched but well-cherished heirloom ornaments collected over the years. In the 1960s, the arbiters of taste recommended choosing a fresh theme every year, and purchasing color-coordinated ornaments for each new season. Those Laura Ingles Wilder girls would have to wait for the 1970s, when another wave of Dickensmania, and a fresh fascination for American country style, brought the classic evergreen back into fashion.

TREE STANDS

Although tree stands began appearing in the 1880s, the first ones weren't greatly better than the home-sawed crossboards and nails that had preceded them. Deeming them not worth the expense, many people invested their money in something showier, like ornaments. By the 1930s, the stands became more stable-looking, but still overlooked one important aspect — safety. The fact that a slowly drying Christmas tree posed a greater fire hazard than one kept moist was overlooked until the 1940s, when stands with water reservoirs began to appear. These were more expensive, and sometimes more elaborate as well. One model typical of the era featured a closed base resembling a large inverted funnel, which was then painted either gold, red, or white and decorated with snowmen, Santas, poinsettas, and other signs of the season.

ORNAMENTS

Homemade tree decorations were the rule of the day until a skeptical Frank Woolworth introduced ready-made German ornaments in 1880. Woolworth's reservations — that customers wouldn't know what to make of them and profits would be eaten up by breakage — proved unfounded. The ornaments sold out in two days, and sold out again the following season. These

Christmas Ornaments..

2⅝-inch fancy
glass balls   12 for $1.41

fragile, hand-cast and hand-painted ornaments were both elaborate and expensive. Taking the form of Santas, teardrops, globes, fruit, pinecones, reindeer, and angels, they were sold not by the box but one at a time, to customers who could only afford one or two new ornaments each year.

Germany dominated the ornament trade until the eve of World War II, when world tensions prompted United States manufacturers to get into the market. Instead of labor-intensive imports, American manufacturers focused on low cost, mass-produced ornaments. With a few modifications, Corning Glass's light-bulb machine could turn out 2,000 plain glass balls a minute, blanks that newly founded ornament companies like Shiny Brite purchased, decorated, and sold by the boxful. Even Harry H. Heim, a manufacturer of hand-blown ornaments, was able to out-produce Germany's cottage-based industry, selling millions of ornaments each year. Heim's ornaments came in simple shapes like the globe and the teardrop, but were still inexpensive enough to be sold by the dozen. There was, however, little color choice, and boxes contained five red ornaments, five green, one gold, and one silver.

What had begun as a stopgap measure became the preferred model. As part of the Marshall Plan, Shiny Brite's founder was sent to Germany after the war to help reestablish the ornament trade, but it was too late — Americans now preferred the mass-produced items that were not only more durable but so inexpensive one could afford an instant collection of glistening, colorful ornaments.

In the postwar world, Max Eckardt's Shiny Brite company took the lead. Packaged in window-paned boxes that offered shoppers a tempting glimpse of the contents, the array was dazzling. With wartime shortages over, gold and silver balls could be produced in large numbers. In addition to traditional red and green, balls also came in other colors, including turquoise, orange, chartreuse, purple, and deep yellow. There were balls with multicolored bands like the rings of Saturn, balls with silk-screened holiday images and messages, and rippled balls that resembled behives. Another typical product was the "reflector" ball, a colored ball with a recessed medallion of silver whose facets caught and reflected the light. By the early 1950s, there were also balls of clear colored glass, decorated with bands of opaque color or sparkling glitter.

Balls weren't the only ornaments to be had, of course. There were also the elongated teardrop and lemon shapes of old, and there were bells that came in all the bright metallics that balls did. There were also ornaments made of that new material, plastic. Because it could be easily poured and molded, thin, lightweight, plastic made excellent snowmen, reindeer, and Santas. Attempts have also been made, over the years, to make balls out of plastic, but with only moderate success. Not everything that can be made unbreakable should be, apparently, at least as far as consumers are concerned and, breakable or not, glass balls have remained popular year in and year out.

Mary: Go on, Pete, you're a big boy. You can put the star up. Way up at the top. That's it.

— **Donna Reed** in *It's a Wonderful Life*, 1946

TREE TOPPERS

The Victorian age, which never saw a straight line it didn't want to improve with a curlicue or bit of decoration, gave us the tree topper, that final ornament perched on the very apex of the tree, adding a few more majestic inches. The earliest toppers were large ornaments, usually in a pendant shape, but stars and angels quickly became equally common. In the 1940s and 1950s, with the introduction of translucent molded plastic, electrified, lit-from-within tree toppers became extremely popular. Although attempts were made to place other Christmas icons — such as Santa — at the top of the tree, stars and angels have remained the kings and queens of the treetop.

RIBBON ICICLES

4 OZ.

Streamline
YOUR
TREE

Extra long

TINSEL

A traditional tree trimming in Europe, tinsel was initially made of filaments of silver and, while long-lasting, was unaffordable to many. By the 1920s, a process had been devised to manufacture shiny silvery tinsel out of lead. Heavier than the real silver that came before, lead tinsel hung in straight, glistening strips — after the yearly task of untangling it, that is — and presented a beautiful sight when dripping from the branches of a tree. Unfortunately, lead proved to be hazardous to the environment as well as to individuals. Toddlers crawling underneath the tree could pull off fistfuls of the shiny stuff and eat it. When disposed of in the household trash, it went into landfills and leaked steadily into the environment. At the end of the 1960s, the United States banned sales of lead tinsel, and tinsel sold in America today is made of lightweight plastic.

ICICLES

Although tinsel was often sold as "icicles" for the tree, there were icicle ornaments as well. One type was metal — narrow, twisted strips of shiny tin on whose sharp edges innumerable little fingers were invariably cut. Another, safer sort was made of plastic. Molded to resemble a five-to-seven-inch icicle with a hook in the top, these came in clear, white, and pale ice blue, the latter two types having glow-in- the-dark capabilities. To children brought up to believe that nothing glowed, glistened, or lit up without electricity, this was nothing short of miraculous.

GARLANDS

In the years before flocked and metal trees arrived, the ideal tree was an evergreen shimmering with tinsel. The problem, as every tree-decorator knows, is that the job of hanging tinsel is almost guaranteed to kill off holiday cheer. Tinsel tangles, it clumps together, and the old-fashioned metal variety was also prone to breakage. When Frank Woolworth discovered a small Philadelphia company that turned imported European tinsel into garlands, he knew he'd found a gold-mine. He bought everything the company could produce and, eventually, persuaded the manufacturer to vastly increase his capacity. Tinsel garlands became an immediate and popular staple — not only for the tree but for banisters, fireplace mantels, and chandeliers. When the war halted access to German tinsel, an American tinsel industry sprang up overnight, due in part to the demand for tinsel garlands. Other ready-made garlands also became popular — ropes of colored chenille, plastic and papier mâché bells, and small glass beads resembling miniature Christmas balls were all common. In the early 1950s, manufacturers began to experiment with that still relatively new miracle product, cellophane, which could be produced in any color imaginable and whose stiff, glossy surface gave of a shimmer not unlike that of tinsel.

ANGEL HAIR

Even in the earliest days of the Christmas tree, people instinctively sought a decoration that might resemble drifts of snow. An early method was to douse the tree with water, followed by a coating of flour. Later, Americans living in the south scattered balls of cotton among the branches. Eventually, homemade efforts were replaced by angel hair, a glistening white substance resembling cotton candy. The drawback was that angel hair was made of spun glass, and whoever had the job of arranging it could count on ending up with red, itchy fingers. No wonder angel hair declined in popularity when flocked trees and aerosol snow came onto the market.

LET THERE BE LIGHTS!

Christmas tree lights have been around almost as long as electricity itself. The first tree festooned with lights was glimpsed in New York City in 1882, the same year the city was electrified. Not surprisingly, the tree resided in the parlor of the

electric company's vice-president. It featured 80 lights that flashed red, white, and blue as the tree revolved and was such a sensation that newspapers across the country commented on it. The White House got its first electrically lit tree three years later, and by the early 1900s the first light sets appeared in stores.

Nevertheless, it was several decades before electric lights became ubiquitous on home trees. For one thing, not everyone had electricity. While most city-dwellers had service by the 1930, only 25% of rural homes had been wired by 1939. Another obstacle was expense. In 1903, a modest 24-socket set that came with 20 plain bulbs, four frosted ones, and four red ones sold for $12 — quite a price when the average wage was just 22¢ an hour. Even department stores found lights expensive, and often rented sets for the season instead of purchasing them outright. Beyond the cost of the sets themselves, there was the added cost of electricity. Early strands of lights featured large, 120-volt bulbs of 5 or 10 watts each. Not only did they use several times as much power as the mini-lights that came later, they generated an enormous amount of heat, posing a fire hazard.

Yet, despite these drawbacks, everyone yearned to have a set of beautiful colored lights with which to adorn the tree. Some modifications — like safety plugs and strings that could be connected to each other — were aimed at making lights safer and easier to use. Others were geared toward novelty and allure. Although the first lights were shaped exactly like a lightbulb, General Electric took the lead in experimenting with alternative shapes, first round and then the cone shape that remained standard through the 1970s. Beautiful figural bulbs also came on the scene. Initially imported from Europe or Japan, these bulbs of painted glass or milk glass took the shape of Santas, angels, bells, dogs, and other fanciful forms. Also popular were "bell" lights, in which a milk glass bell surrounding the bulb was decorated with characters and signs of the season.

One of the first to incorporate popular culture into the mix was NOMA, which in 1935 produced a set of bell lights that featured Mickey Mouse and other Walt Disney characters. NOMA (an acronym for the National Outfit Manufacturer's Association) had been founded as a trade association of smaller manufacturers and began selling lights under its own name in the 1920s. By 1940 it had emerged as a premiere name in holiday lights. If you decorated a tree, a home, or even a tabletop anytime between 1930 and 1965, chances are you used a NOMA product. NOMA's designers were endlessly inventive, and in addition to lights, the company made electric candles and candelabra, illuminated wreaths and Santa faces for the front door, tree-topping angels and stars, Santas, choir boys and snowmen for the yard, and tabletop decorations such as white plastic churches and musical altars. In 1940 the company introduced a clear plastic halo that, when placed around the base of a light, gave off a candle-like shimmer. The next year it debuted a tabletop tree whose individually lit branches were a vast improvement over previous models, which were lit from within by a single bulb. The war interrupted the flow of nonstop whimsey, and new designs were put on hold for the duration. After V-J Day, however, the designers went back to work and brought out one of the most successful novelties of all time.

It's not known who first thought of filling a small, candle-like glass tube with colored liquid which, when heated by a small light, would bubble away merrily. Whoever it was deserves a place in the inventor's hall of fame, for there's scarcely a post-war child who doesn't have a fond memory of these novelty lights. NOMA appears to be the first company to manufacture Bubble Lites, bringing them to the market in 1946. Patents for similar items were granted to other inventors around the same time, and by the next season numerous other companies were also offering the bubblers.

In the rush to make Christmas ever bigger and brighter, no one company ever had the lighting market to itself, and competition was fierce. The same year NOMA introduced Bubbler Lites, Sylvania introduced fluorescent pastel lights, a move that anticipated the shimmering, pearlized fad of the 1960s. In 1955, NOMA marketed its first set of flashing lights. Three years later, GE introduced Lighted Ice Bulbs, spherical blue bulbs covered with candy-like "ice" crystals. Perhaps the biggest innovation of the postwar

years — certainly the most influential — came from abroad. In 1950, the Fairy Light was imported from Italy, proving so popular it was quickly followed by similar entries from Germany, Holland, Japan, and several American companies.

Be it known that John Petry, a citizen of the United States and resident of New York City, in the county of Queens, State of New York, has invented a new, original, and ornamental Design for an Illuminable Bubbling Device or the like, of which the following is a specification . . .

— U.S. Patent for a Bubbler Light, 1948

Fairy Lights sounded a death knell for old-style bulbs, and soon morphed into the mini-lights which, by the 1970s, had become the preferred standard in Christmas lighting. In addition to being attractive in themselves, small lights were also less expensive to buy and to run, requiring less electricity than the larger lights. More important, perhaps, was the safety factor. Because the tiny lights generated almost no heat, they posed no threat to tinsel, paper, and boughs of drying evergreens. There was one small drawback, however. Old-style bulbs had been of the simple screw-in variety, making replacement easy. Early mini-lights were wired together on the same strand, and when one bulb blew out, the whole strand went dark. Children of the 1960s undoubtedly remember the hours of fun to be had as the whole family sat around testing each tiny light to locate the source of the problem.

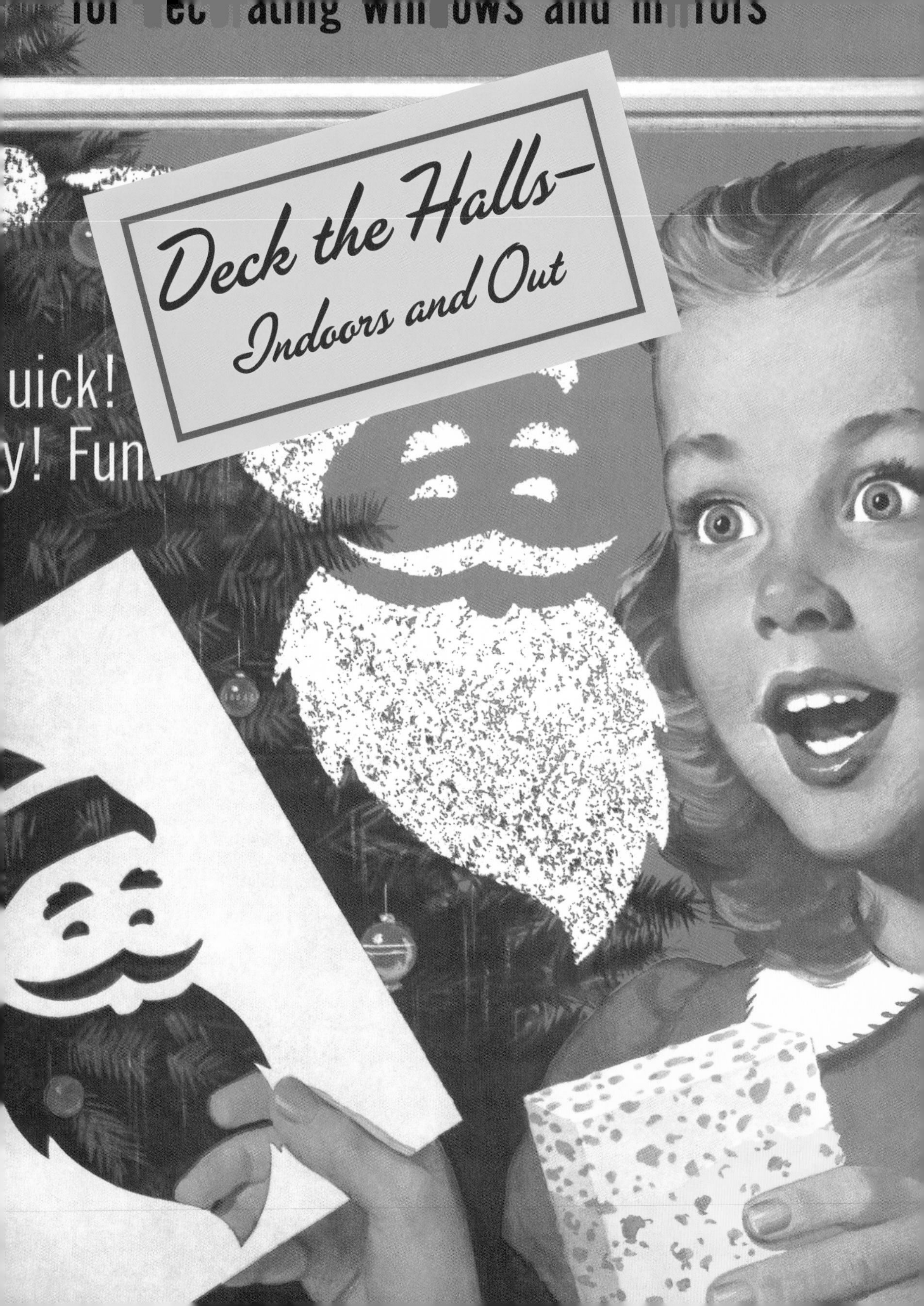
Deck the Halls—
Indoors and Out

The tree, of course was only the beginning. As the variety of manufactured decorations grew along with the consumer's ability to afford them, Christmas decorating became a cellar to rooftop event. Each year, manufacturers responded to the previous season's demand by creating ever more holiday items, challenging shoppers to find places for all the things they wanted to buy.

The earliest manufactured decorations were simple and inexpensive — red and green paper steamers to adorn archways and door lintels, and red and white honeycomb bells to hang from them. Everyone could afford these penny pleasures, and having something "store bought" when so many items were still home-made added a sense of luxury to the season.

It was not long, however, until more elaborate items became available. The fireplace mantel, a common feature of most homes built in the early part of the 20th century, served as a natural focal point and display area. Nativity scenes were extremely popular. For little more than a dollar, one could buy a

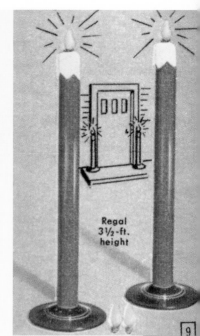

Regal
3½-ft.
height

9

cardboard set that came with a few plastic figures or, for ten times that, an illuminated set that came with two dozen figures and music box accompaniment.

14

The late 1940s and early 1950s witnessed a special passion for electric, illuminated plug-in decorations that could be diplayed on a mantel or tabletop. Electric candoliers allowed people to enjoy the illusion of "old-fashioned" decor at its modern best, without the fear of fire or the mess of dripping wax. In addition to candles there were illuminated Santas, angels, snowmen, choir boys, and white plastic red-roofed churches, whose translucent windows transformed the light of an ordinary bulb into a peaceful, mystical glow. There were miniature trees that lit up and played music, and tiered musical altars of ivory plastic trimmed with gold. For the windows, there were small bottlebrush wreaths with electric candles in the center.

Plastic and electrically lit display pieces lost favor in the 1960s. They looked out of place and a bit tacky in the new, sleekly modern houses built in the post-war boom, and many were packed away until grown children, searching for memories, unpacked them years later. Decorations of the 1960s were spare and modern, emphasizing natural elements, streamlined style, and functionality. The lighted plastic church of the '50s gave way to the silver bowl piled with monochromatic balls. The console stereo displayed stylized reindeer in silver or brass. Crystal or frosted glass candlesticks replaced the plastic candoliers, and the mantel-less fireplace was bare except for a basket of logs and pine cones.

HOMEMADE BECOMES HANDCRAFTED

Before manufactured goods became the norm, the majority of tree ornaments and other decorations were homemade. The advent of purchased items didn't put an end to homemade efforts, but simply made them an elective activity. Now that you didn't have to make everything yourself, making a few select things became enjoyable and even artistic. Plain and unexciting "homemade" goods suddenly became "handcrafted" heirlooms.

Purchased Christmas stockings were one of the last manufactured items to catch fire with the public, as most children had stockings lovingly made by mothers, grandmothers, or aunts. Companies like Simplicity and McCalls sold patterns for stockings. Embroidery or appliqué work

were the usual adornments, along with beads, sequins, and names spelled out in festive glitter. Appliquéd and embroidered towels, aprons, and tree skirts were also favorite projects. For the time-pressed there were iron-on prints, which transferred colored motifs onto fabric and

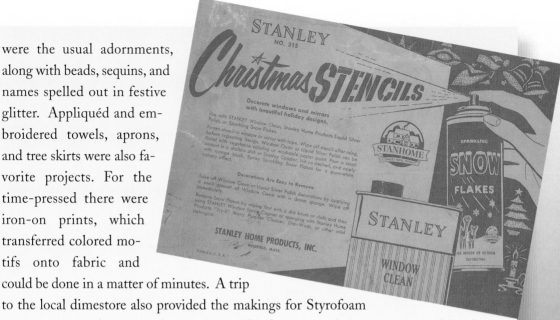

could be done in a matter of minutes. A trip to the local dimestore also provided the makings for Styrofoam snowmen, pipe-cleaner reindeer and elves, felt Santas, beaded ornaments, and hand-painted manger scenes. Children lucky enough to have a mother or grandmother who crocheted could look forward to lacy snowflakes stiched of white thread and dipped in heavy starch to stiffen them.

The most popular project, however, was also the simplest, and the average age of the participants was firmly in the single digits. For children, windows were a magical blank canvas just waiting to be decorated. Construction paper cutouts of snowflakes, Santas, and Christmas trees were all very well, but for sheer fun they couldn't compete with window stencils. Someone had discovered that Glass Wax, a cleaner which dried to a nice opaque white if left on long enough, could be used in place of paint to stencil all manner of holiday motifs onto windows. Seeing Santa's face or the words "Merry Christmas" appear on your very own window was magical, and kids whose mothers were artistic enough to add a few drops of food coloring had the added satisfaction of being able to go Technicolor with green wreaths, red sleighs, and pale blue angels. Best of all, when the season was over, all mom had to do was wipe the stuff away.

Just as the novelty of working with Glass Wax was beginning to wear thin, aerosol snow came along in the mid-1950s and gave the whole adventure new appeal. Christmas window stencils remained ubiquitous from the 1950s through the 1960s. In addition to stencil sets, there were stencil books and numerous premium giveaways, including a set of Howdy Doody Christmas stencils.

A VERY EISENHOWER CHRISTMAS

During their years in the White House, the Eisenhowers did Christmas on a grand scale. For the 1958 holiday season, Mamie arranged for carols to be piped into every room. Miles of greenery were wrapped around every column, indoors and out, and over two dozen trees were decorated in classic 1950s style, with glass balls, electric candle lights, and waterfalls of tinsel.

THE GREAT OUTDOORS

World War II made permanent changes in the homefront. Returning soldiers who'd never before thought of leaving the farms and rural towns of their birth now — having marched through Europe or been to the South Pacific — thought nothing of moving across the continent. They had new skills, courtesy of Uncle Sam, and there were dozens of new industries waiting to employ them. During the 1950s alone, America converted over five million acres of land to new homes. Suburbia had been born.

The shining promise of the suburbs was that every homeowner could preside over his own little domain, so long as he paid his mortgage on time. Between mom and dad, this quickly became an indoor-outdoor split, with dad taking command of the yard, the patio and deck, and the grill. It was only a matter of time until the simple wreath on the door was replaced by a winter wonderland of blinking, flashing, revolving, and sometimes musical outdoor decorations.

It started modestly enough, with lights around the eaves. To be honest, the suburbs needed a decorative touch. Far from the commercial district, with nothing even remotely like a downtown area, mile upon mile of tract housing could look a bit monotonous. Homes hadn't been in place long enough to acquire distinctive additions and remodels. Many streets, built on old farm fields, still lacked sidewalks, and having a tree taller than 10 feet was a luxury. So when dad came home from Sears or Montgomery Ward with lights that blinked and a large, lit-from-within Santa face for the front door, it was a very big deal.

It was a very big deal for the guy across the street, too, who did his neighbor one better by framing his house with lights and wrapping lights around every tree in the front yard. Then the guy down the street astounded his family by ordering a set of giant illuminated candles to flank the front door, which turned out to be not nearly as flashy as

his neighbor's almost life-size carolers on the front lawn. There is no doubt that competitiveness played a large role in outdoor decoration. Men who would not ordinarily stir from the television set on weekends suddenly mounted ladders to wrap the entire house in lights and affix illuminated sleighs and reindeer to the roof. Front lawn crèche scenes rivaled those of churches. Newspaper stories appeared about the whopping electric bills some homeowners ran up during the month of December.

Over the years, outdoor decorations put up by private homeowners not only matched public and commercial displays but, in some cases, eclipsed them as a drawing card. Local papers in virtually every city published guides to the best-decorated homes. For many families, piling in the car and driving from neighborhood to neighborhood to browse the lights while carols played on the radio became a new Christmas tradition, sometimes carried out on Christmas Eve in hopes of distracting the kids for the last few hours before the presents were handed out.

If aliens could look in on households at Christmastime, they would see people wrapping items in paper, gathering together to exchange items, and then indulging in a mad orgy of unwrapping the items that were carefully wrapped just hours — or minutes — before. No doubt they would conclude that Earthlings are mad. Especially if they also got wind of the blizzard of greeting cards and gift tags, the miles of ribbon and the stadiums full of bows that also accompany the holiday. Christmas has always been a paper-intensive holiday, and few of us would willingly give up the suspense and excitement of the mysterious packages and bright, curling ribbons that add so much color and pattern to the season.

CHRISTMAS CARDS AND LETTERS

Inexpensive long-distance rates, email, an increase in all-occasion cards, and the press of modern life have taken their toll on that one-time must, the Christmas card. At the dawn of the 21st century, Americans send and receive far fewer cards than they did fifty years earlier. In 1958, when mailed cards reached an all-time per capita peak, the average American family sent out a hundred season's greetings — three to four times as many cards as the average household sends out today.

In fact, the modern Christmas card was marketed as a way to simplify life, not complicate it. At the turn of the century, the sudden availability of inexpensive, factory-made goods inspired a tide of obligatory gift-giving. Each year, people bought and received more and more token gifts, an investment of time and money that soon proved burdensome to all. Card companies positioned Christmas cards as an alternative to the mounting tide of unwanted bedroom slippers,

Greetings

vanity cases, kimonos, and celluloid collars, and a new tradition was born. Between 1905 and 1915, Hallmark, Gibson, American Greetings, and Norcross all went into business.

Even so, the "classic American card" had yet to be born. From the start of the century through the early 1920s, Christmas postcards were far more common than Christmas cards. And it was only gradually that seasonal motifs such as Santas, wrapped presents, and snowy scenes replaced the lace, flowers, and filigree of Victorian cards. The folded-style card, with art on the outside and text within, gained popularity throughout the opulent 1920s, and, as printing techniques improved, art became an increasingly important part of the package. Yet the new, more lavishly styled cards proved unaffordable for many after the Crash of 1929.

Two staples of mid-century card-giving arose as a direct result of the Depression — the Christmas letter and the family photo. People who had gotten into the habit of sending cards didn't want to stop simply because times were hard. Instead, they began writing special Christmas letters, summing up the family's activities and achievements over the past year. Paper manufacturers responded by printing sheets of stationary decorated with poinsettias, candles, ribbon borders, and snowy scenes. Especially popular from the late 1940s on was the custom of sending family snapshots, which were relatively inexpensive yet, printed on flat cards with season's greetings, still managed to look special.

THE 1940S

World War II heralded a golden age of card giving. With so many husbands and sons overseas and families and friends separated by thousands of miles, Christmas correspondance took on a special poignancy. The whimsical cards of the previous decades gave rise to comforting scenes of snow-covered homes, fire-lit hearths, and everyday life. Patriotic themes were common, and even traditional motifs were often colored in red-white-and-blue. Servicemen and women stationed at dozens of U.S. bases could receive standard-weight cards and letters, but mail being shipped across oceans had to be as lightweight as possible. On the homefront, stationary companies printed tissue-thin paper and envelopes decorated with a blend of Christmas and military themes. For those in the service, there was stationary printed with the names of battalions and divisions, bearing motifs of exotic locales and vague, security-conscious reminders that the letter came "from the Middle East" or "somewhere in Europe."

After 1945, although many service personnel remained stationed overseas, Christmas cards lost their military overtones. Once again there were snowy scenes of overflowing mailboxes and beribboned front doors, and a sudden nostalgia for the 19th century sprouted Currier-and-Ives-style scenes of sleighs and carolers. Cards, printed on thick four-fold paper, regained the modestly luxurious look and feel they'd had before the war. Although a wide array could be purchased in boxed sets from stores, one now-forgotten feature of the late 1940s and early 1950s was the door-to-door card salesman who would arrive in early autumn, his samples glued to a trifold cardboard display, and take orders for cards that would be personalized with the sender's name.

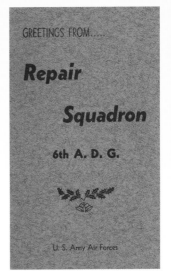

When You Care Enough to Send the Very Best

— One of the best-known ad slogans of all time penned by Hallmark executive Ed Goodman, 1944

THE 1950S

During the war, Christmas cards and letters had been sent to family back home. After the war, they were needed to keep track of service pals and friends who'd relocated to other parts of the country. Understandably, the 1950s set records for Christmastime correspondence. Washington joined in the trend, and in 1953 White House cards were sent out for the first time. President Eisenhower, an amateur artist, consulted personally with the president of Hallmark about the cards, and to this day no administration has issued such a variety of designs. Over two terms, the Eisenhower White House issued 38 different cards and prints, many of them bearing the President's own artwork.

Even the Korean War and nuclear jitters couldn't cast too much of a shadow over what proved to be one of the most prosperous and reassuring decades in American history, and cards from this time reflect both the new domesticity and a new confidence in a distinctly American culture. Early in the decade, cards were cozy and sincere, still flush with the wonder of having come through a depression and a world war. By mid-decade, people felt comfortable enough to poke fun at the brave new world they were living in. The studio or "slim jim" card, a tall, narrow card with streamlined art and a humorous punch line, made its debut. Santa was pulled out of his traditional sleigh and shown arriving in a huge tail-finned car, beatniks delivered season's greetings in hep cat lingo.

With so many people to keep in touch with, and so many people getting down to the postwar business of raising families, it's no wonder that two types of correspondence were especially common during these years — the photo card and the family newsletter. For people who hadn't seen each other since V-J day, and probably wouldn't see each other for several more years, the photo card was a quick and relatively painless way of staying in touch. The family newsletter was another matter. In the days before computers, when Xerox machines were still rare and generally inaccessible, the family newsletter was a major project, requiring someone (usually mom) to arduously copy, either by hand or typewriter, each letter to be sent out.

THE 1960S

Cards in the 1960s became more sophisticated, more design-focused, and less stereotyped than they had been in the past. Hallmark, which had been producing Hanukkah cards since the 1940s, introduced cards that reflected African-American culture. The warm and cozy card of the 1950s, in vibrant primary colors, was likely to be supplanted by a pastel watercolor of a woodland scene, or a simple embossed gold triangle representing a thoroughly modern Christmas tree. Studio cards continued to be popular and continued to poke fun at world events and American fads. Santa dodging space debris, elves sporting Beatles haircuts, and Christmas trees in psychedelic, Warhol-style colors were typical of the decade.

In the White House, the Kennedys continued the previous administration's custom of sending out Christmas cards. The First Lady even kept up the tradition of First Family artwork — in 1963, a card based on one of her paintings was issued to raise money for a national center for the performing arts. A less happy history belongs to the official White House card of that year. Showing a creche scene, the printed cards arrived at the White House in November, but the President and First Lady had only had time to sign about 500 of them before their tragic trip to Dallas. The few signed cards became valuable and highly sought after by collectors.

CHRISTMAS STAMPS AND SEALS

Two things we take for granted on holiday mail today — Christmas stamps and Christmas seals — both had a bit of a struggle establishing themselves. Many felt that Christmas seals, which date from the first decade of the 20th century, were inappropriate because they linked a sacred holiday with a virulent disease. These ob-

jections were overridden by the public's desire to help stamp out tuberculosis which had affected so many, and the seals soon became a success. This success, however, was no help whatsoever when the postal system proposed printing a special holiday stamp. Other countries had been issuing

Christmas stamps since the eve of the Second World War, but the United States didn't propose one until the early 1960s. The idea met with immediate opposition from those who felt it was a violation of the separation between church and state but the protest

died out and America's first Christmas postage stamp was issued in 1962. The small square stamps, showing a wreath and candles in traditional red and green, proved popular with the card-sending public, and Christmas stamps, featuring a new design each season, have been issued every year since.

"TAPE CHRISTMAS CARDS on your tree with loops of cellophane tape," says Bing. "Pick out cards from your best pals—guys and gals likely to drop in to your diggin's during the holidays. You'll get a big kick out of the grins whe they see their cards on your 'Friendship Tree'!"

BING CROSBY TRIMS A "FRIENDSHIP TREE"

Star of "MR. MUSIC," a Paramount picture, joins in a growing Christmas custom

"A 'FRIENDSHIP TREE' is a wonderful idea," says Nancy Olson, Bing's Paramount co-star. "It gives Christmas greetings extra meaning. All my friends are having a 'Friendship Tree' this year."

"BRIGHTEN UP YOUR HOME with cards taped around the fireplace ar doorways and mirrors," says Nancy. Taped singly or in chains, these colorf Christmas greetings give the whole house a festive look.

EASY TO DO—Take a five-inch strip of "Scotch" Cellophane Tape and press one end of the tape *firmly* on the card. Then ...

PASS TAPE OVER TWIG and stick the other end tightly to the back of the card. Cellophane tape sticks without moistening.

MAKE CHAINS OF CARDS this way. Tape en of chain to molding or woodwork, never to wal paper or painted walls.

WRAP IT UP

There is no one single theory as to why we wrap Christmas gifts, but mercantilism certainly played a part. In the second half of the 19th century, store owners discovered that placing ordinary items, such as pens and handkerchiefs, in specially decorated boxes, persuaded customers to buy them as Christmas gifts. The custom of leaving gifts under the tree also helped, and by the early 1880s wrapping gifts was standard procedure.

Initially, gift wrap was fairly simple. Boxes were either plain pasteboard or pasteboard printed with sprigs of holly. Wrapping paper was initially plain white tissue or letter-weight paper, although by the end of the first decade of the new century red, green, and holly-sprigged tissue was also available. Packages were tied either with tinsel cord or red ribbons. Before adhesive tape was commercially available, in 1932, edges were held together with decorative gummed seals. Decorated paper as we know it today came about

During her eight years as First Lady, Mamie Eisenhower not only personally shopped for gifts for the White House staff but wrapped each one herself to save money.

accidentally, when Hall Brother's store in Kansas City ran out of tissue during the holiday rush and sold sheets of decorated paper meant to be used as envelope lining. At a dime a sheet the paper was a hit. The next year the store sold it at alongside the tissue paper, and discovered that many customers preferred it. The Halls, founders of the Hallmark company, soon began manufacturing their own holiday wrap.

In the 1920s and 1930s, gift wrap (or "gift dressing," as it was then called), came in elaborate sets, complete with tinsel cord and matching gift tags. Colors were rich or metallic, and the holly sprigs of old were replaced by bold stripes, plaids, and checkerboards. Seals were of embossed foil or decorated with holly, Santas, and other Christmas themes. While one might expect the Depression of the 1930s to have made for more modest wrappings, the opposite was true. Wrap remained cheerful and elaborate, possibly to offset the frugality of the gift it concealed.

Add Glamour to your Christmas

Wrap Gifts in Cellophane

DU PONT
Cellophane

During the 1940s, wartime paper shortages put an end to the lavish, heavy wrap of the previous decade, and paper became very thin. Although still printed with holiday motifs, it was so lightweight it often tore on sharp corners, prompting many to come up with homemade alternatives — kitchen gifts wrapped in dishtowels, a bottle of perfume wrapped in a pretty scarf, a new pipe or bottle of aftershave tucked into the toe of dad's new slippers. Since weight was an issue for gifts going overseas, these homemade wrappings were strictly for the homefront.

Interestingly enough, the end of the war did not prompt a return to the elaborate sets of coordinated wrap and tags of earlier years. Although wrapping paper did become heavier and more color-saturated once again, buyers were encouraged to mix and match paper, ribbons, and tags to come up with something unique. Shoppers were encouraged to wrap their own gifts and to be creative about it, to make the gift's external covering a work of art — or, if not quite art, a work of individual expression. Companies like Hallmark, Gibson, and Dennison published booklets full of creative tips. Articles in women's magazines suggested that families that wrapped together had more fun and enjoyed Christmas more.

Many households kept boxes not only of paper and ribbon but of pipe cleaners, construction paper, glitter, glue, and pictures cut from last year's cards. Manufacturers added to their options. Miniature chenille snowmen and angels, small Santas, bells, artificial holly sprigs, and gilded plastic toys and musical instruments were sold as tie-ons. Companies that made adhesive tape introduced opaque varieties in bright colors, stamped with holly, bells, and other motifs, which could not only seal a package but decorate it as well. There were gummed stars in metallic gold, silver, red, and green. Among the most curious add-ons were boxes of thin, transparent colored plastic straws. When tied tightly in the middle, a small bundle of straws made a festive adornment or, when carefully trimmed, pulled, and fanned, produced something that looked vaguely like Sputnik.

As life became busier in the 1960s and many women who had been home with young children in the 1950s joined the work force, the "self-expressive" wrap job was on the decline. Gifts could still be wrapped at home, but they shouldn't look like it. A more polished look came into favor, with wider, satiny type ribbon replacing the curling ribbon of old. Premade bows became more common (anyone who has ever tried to make a good-looking bow with satin ribbon will understand why), and well-dressed packages were meant to reflect the sleek, modern, streamlined look of the times. Packages "cluttered" with seals, glitter, ties-ons, yards of ribbon curls, and other personal touches were out of fashion — and much missed by children who by and large preferred the gaudy, jingle-jangle of the 1950s to the restrained silvers and pale blues of the 1960s.

Christmas Magic

for your gifts, for home decorating . . .

with the shining new excitement of

"SCOTCH" Brand Gift Wrap Tapes

Gay new patterns in "SCOTCH" Gift Wrap Tapes—solid colors, patterns, "metallics"—help make exciting tape-it-easy designs! The trees are swirls of tape with the sticky side out, glitter-sprinkled. Shirt box complete with buttons 'n bow, the stocking, candy cane, and red-headed angel are all made with Gift Wrap Tape, too.

Tape your Christmas wis on a picture window wit the new "SCOTCH" Gift Wra Tapes. Try this stick-at-i touch magic on windows an mirrors all over the house. make a friendly "Friendsh Tree", tape your nicest Chris mas cards to the tree wit "SCOTCH" Cellophane Tap

For those who think Christmas has only recently gotten too commercial, think again. Judging by the volume of cranky protest about it, Christmas has always been too commercial. Store ads urging shoppers to buy for the holiday season began appearing in America in the very early 1800s, even though Christmas then was still a relatively private holiday, celebrated more with food and drink than with luxurious gifts. As the volume of manufactured goods and the incomes to afford them rose, so did stores' efforts to sell them. It didn't take retailers long to figure out that Christmas was an opportune time to do this, and that a short, intense burst of frenzied selling could make a lean year fat and fat year golden. Macy's department store in New York observed its first open-until-midnight Christmas Eve in 1867, and sold $6,000 worth of merchandise. By the end of the 19th century, the retail season revolved around December and Christmas was inextricably linked with shopping and spending.

Was this much-criticized plunge toward commercialism all bad? Not if you were a clerk, manufacturer, ad writer, or sales representative. Not if your job was in some way

connected with designing and producing the millions of goods sold in thousands of stores across the country. During the Depression, it was the income of the holiday season that allowed many store-owners to survive.

A more subtle benefit of commercialization is offered by Penne Restad in *Christmas in America*. In a multicultural country that promises freedom of religious choice, emphasizing the commercial aspects of Christmas over the religious ones was a practical way of including everyone. After all, Santa never asks a child who or what he believes in.

Of course, the retail world had no such altruistic aims in mind. Their concern was in selling as many sleds, baby dolls, rocking horses, boxes of chocolate, bottles of perfume, and neckties as possible, and to this end they were willing to pull out all the stops. For good or ill, retail commerce is an entrenched part of Christmas, and one curmudgeon's lamentation about Santa the salesman is another person's happy childhood memory.

WHY CHRISTMAS STARTS WITH THANKSGIVING

American retailers were up against a unique challenge. Falling at the end of November, Thanksgiving, with its football rivalries, quiet family gatherings, and emphasis on *gratitude* rather than *wanting* was antithetical to the whole commercial ideal. Yet such a major holiday, and one so thoroughly American, could hardly be bumped aside. The solution was to Christmas-ize Thanksgiving, and make it the official starting gun for a flat-out rush to the stores.

In 1920, Gimbel's department store in New York organized the first Thanksgiving parade, the highlight of which was a fireman hired to dress as Santa Claus. Other stores around the nation quickly followed suit. In Detroit, Hudson's started the Santa's Thanksgiving Day Parade in 1924, and that same year, back in New York, the Macy's Thanksgiving Day Parade got its start. With Santa arriving in the very last float, Christmas — and the shopping season — was officially underway. Since many people had the next day off, store owners made the Friday after Thanksgiving a sort of national shopping day, with special sales, special hours, and special attractions to lure customers. In most American cities, the Friday after Thanksgiving became the day when downtown shopping districts turned on their holiday lights and stores unveiled their Christmas windows.

So important did the intense, month–long burst of Christmas-related shopping become to the national economic well-being that, in 1939, when Thanksgiving fell on the last day of a five-Thursdayed November, Federated Department Stores protested the shortened shopping season. President Roosevelt moved the holiday up a week, thus adding six days to the shopping season. In 1941, Congress passed a bill officially moving Thanksgiving from the "last Thursday" in November to the "fourth Thursday," ensuring that there would always be a maximum number of shopping days.

DEPARTMENT STORES

In today's world of specialty shops, discount superstores, and online browsing, it's hard to imagine the role the department store once played in American life. Each town had one of these emporiums, housing thousands of square feet of merchandise beneath a single roof. Located in the town's central shopping district, the department store served as a kind of town square. Wealthy people could not go to a "better" store, and poor and middle-class people would not be turned away. As an economic blender, it was a great homogenizer.

Department stores also played a unique role at Christmastime. Because their budgets, floor space, and potential profits were so much larger than smaller shops, they took the lead in marketing Christmas as an in-store event. It cost a quarter to go to the movies, but for free one could linger for hours over fantasy windows, spectacular toylands, mechanized villages, and red–suited Santas, all set against the backdrop of alluring and highly desirable merchandise. Whole families trooped downtown each year to enjoy these retail spectacles, and a new annual tradition became part of millions of American lives.

Retailers realized early on that windows made ideal picture frames for their merchandise. In the 1920s, Christmas windows took a revolutionary turn. Ed Dean, display manager for Dayton's department store in Minneapolis, began designing windows that were whimsical rather than merely merchandise-filled. Although Macy's in New York had long incorporated merchandise into various window themes, Dean's windows skipped the merchandise altogether. Among his creations were mechanical cutouts illustrating scenes from *The Rubaiyat* of Omar Khayyam, a life-size elephant that swung its trunk and swished its tail, and tableaux of circus acts and nursery rhymes. The idea was to give the windows a new theme each year, and to make each season's offering grander and more alluring than the year before. One year it was dolls, another the circus, still another nursery rhyme characters.

Soon other stores adopted the merchandise–free strategy, and fantasy windows became the rule of the day. In 1946, Marshall Field's in Chicago used its long parade of windows to tell the story of *The Night Before Christmas* from start to finish, which proved so popular with shoppers that the store offered the public a new story every year thereafter. In cities across America, each season's store windows became an annual news event, and town residents turned out to see the show. The amount of free advertising, customer good will, foot traffic, and attention from the retail world was enormous.

Why are holiday windows invariably secular? Has commercialism completely drowned out Christmas's true origins? It turns out the opposite is true — retailers have always been cautious of anything that might seem to exploit religion. In 1952, to satisfy customers who'd requested a nativity display, Dayton's in Minneapolis created a sacred side of the store, keeping it separate from the Santas, sleigh bells, toy soldiers and decorated trees that enlivened the rest of the store.

Windows were by no means the only investment retailers made. Awnings garlanded with holly, Santas and sleighs climbing store roofs, interior pillars wrapped with pine, elaborately decorated Christmas trees and Santa villages and Toylands — all these were important in setting the holiday mood. Marshall Field's, in Chicago, was a leader in cellar-to-ceiling decorating. In the 1940s, instead of having windows to delight

SONGS OF THE SEASON

For centuries revelers sang solemn carols. Then something exciting happened. Electricity. The radio. Movies. A booming record industry. It was an explosion of sound, usually mushrooming around the ears of holiday shoppers. Here are a few of the bright new songs that kept buyers in a merry mood.

1942 "White Christmas"

1942 "Happy Holiday"

1943 "I'll Be Home For Christmas"

1944 "Have Yourself a Merry Little Christmas"

1945 "Let It Snow"

1946 "The Christmas Song"

1946 "All I Want For Christmas Is My Two Front Teeth"

1947 "Here Comes Santa Claus"

1948 "Caroling Caroling"

1949 "It's a Marshmallow World"

1949 "Mele Kelikimaka"

1949 "Rudolph the Red-Nosed Reindeer"

1949 "Blue Christmas"

1950 "Frosty the Snowman"

1950 "Silver Bells"

1950 "Sleigh Ride"

1950 "There's No Christmas Like a Home Christmas"

1951 "It's Beginning To Look a Lot Like Christmas"

1952 "I Saw Mommy Kissing Santa Claus"

1953 "Santa Baby"

1954 "The Christmas Waltz"

1954 "(There's No Place Like) Home for the Holidays"

1955 "Nuttin' For Christmas"

1957 "Jingle-Bell Rock"

1957 "The Little Drummer Boy"

1958 "Rockin' Around the Christmas Tree"

1958 "The Chipmunk Song"

1962 "A Holly Jolly Christmas"

1962 "Do You Hear What I Hear?"

1963 "Pretty Paper"

1963 "It's the Most Wonderful Time of the Year"

the children and decorations of various sorts in different departments, Field's designers began decorating the whole store around a single theme. This required not only ingenuity but massive effort as well — the store estimated that some 4,000 employees were required to complete the decorations each year. The effect was dazzling, and people who might before have been content to see only the windows and the main floor now became interested in seeing the whole store, and as they walked through each floor they invariably made purchases.

The 1950s and 1960s were the heyday of downtown windows, with stores striving each season to surpass their previous year's efforts and those of their competitors. Stores that had kept their windows dark on Sundays began to light them up. Eventually, by the mid-1960s, states started to repeal their Sunday closing laws, and stores began to keep limited Sunday hours.

After the 1960s, while large stores could still be counted on for interesting and delightful windows, soaring costs caused many retailers to scale back their efforts, to recycle decorations from one season to another, or rely on rented window decorations. An even bigger factor may have been that new feature on the American landscape, the suburban shopping mall. With branches of the main store located in the customer's own neighborhood, there was no reason to lure shoppers downtown, and the advent of sophisticated attractions like color television, animated movies, television specials, and later VCRs and DVDs, made children just a little less excited about the prospect of pacing a long line of windows in the cold.

THE SANTA SHOT

Retail Santas began appearing during the Civil War, working primarily as promotion men and greeters who welcomed customers to the store. In 1890, James Edgar of the Boston Store in Brockton, Massachusetts, installed Santa in his own Santa Land domain and introduced him to the younger set, whose wishes and wants he listened to for hours on end. Macy's, in New York, followed suit, and by the beginning of the 20th century Santa had become a huge drawing card for little people everywhere.

The competition was fierce and, as lines and waiting times grew, stores searched for ways to induce parents and children to choose their store over their competitor's. If Gimble's put Santa on a silver throne, Macy's gave him one of gold. If Gimble's retaliated with a golden throne the following season, Macy's would get him a sleigh and reindeer. By the 1940s and '50s, most store Santas presided over their own Toy Lands or Santa Lands or Christmas Cottages, where Mrs. Santa and a crew of Santa's helpers doled out free candy canes and

booklets of Christmas songs and stories. For parents, there was the promise of shortened wait times, a trick accomplished by clever set design. By creating a maze-like Santa's workshop with more than one Santa room, multiple Santas could work simultaneously in identical rooms, leaving each child certain that he or she had seen the one and only Mr. Claus. Marshall Field's Cozy Cloud Cottage had four such Santa nooks, while Hudson's, in downtown Detroit, could keep the laps of six Santas simultaneously filled with children.

In addition to shorter waiting times, retailers also used technology to attract parents. At mid-century, the snapshot was still a relatively new plaything, and many people had yet to acquire cameras that could accommodate flashbulbs, which had come on the market in the 1930s. Yet what parent wouldn't want a picture of Sis and Junior perched on Santa's lap? The idea took off, and soon the Santa shot was a standard offering in almost every department store in America. For a modest sum, mom and dad could have a permanent reminder of the visit, usually framed in a special display folder bearing the store's name. In some families, the annual Santa shot joined the school picture as a record of each child's progress from tiny tot to Santa skeptic. Of course, the long lines, the discomfort of standing around in overheated stores swathed in woolly coats and slush-spattered boots, combined with the sheer tension of not knowing whether or not the special toy would arrive, didn't make for a universally cheerful crew, and many pictures in family archives show tots in various stages of mood discontent. *Oh look, there's little Pete pulling Santa's beard off!*

As with downtown windows, the golden age of the store Santa began to decline with the rise of the shopping mall. Creating a maze with four cleverly concealed Santas was one thing, but explaining how the one true Santa could be at all of the mall's major stores at once was another matter. And, with less floor space available and economy of the essence, stores found it financially more practical to let a single, centrally located mall Santa listen patiently to the thousands of whispered wishes and wants of young customers.

MOVE OVER SANTA: RUDOLPH MANIA STRIKES MONTGOMERY WARD

In 1939, with the Depression still casting a shadow over sales and war worries depressing the general mood, executives at Montgomery Ward were looking for a special Christmas draw to lure shoppers. Traditional themes — Santa, *The Night Before Christmas*, Dickens's *A Christmas Carol*, the Twelve Days of Christmas — all seemed a bit tired, and not nearly distinctive enough. They appealed to Robert May, a company copy-

writer, to come up with a whole new take on Christmas. May responded with a story poem whose meter and opening lines seem borrowed from Clement Moore's famous work.

> *'Twas the day before Christmas and*
> *all through the hills*
> *The reindeer were playing, enjoying the spills . . .*

The similarities soon fade, and May's poem emerges as a beguiling and wholly unique tale of a left-out, overlooked reindeer who against all odds ends up literally outshining his fellows. Montgomery Ward printed the poem in book form, with illustrations by art department employee Denver Gillen, and gave out 2.5 million copies over the Christmas season.

Instead of fading with the season's wrapping paper, Rudolph lingered in the popular

Although May early on decided he wanted an alliterative name for his Red-Nosed Reindeer, finding the right one took a while. May considered Rollo, which he rejected as too carefree, and Reginald, which seemed too British, before settling on Rudolph.

conscious. May had created the perfect icon for the era. Rudolph, the bashful, small, unappreciated reindeer who becomes a hero, was a character with which every child could identify. Who has not felt rejected and left out at some point? And what child has not dreamed of doing something so spectacular even his worst enemies would come to admire him? For parents, the story's American virtues — rooting for the underdog, the importance of every individual, and the belief that doing one's best will be rewarded — seemed all the more poignant against the backdrop of Hitler's war machine. Due to paper shortages, Montgomery Ward could not reissue the story during World War II. But when it brought the story back in 1946, another 3.6 million copies went into eager young hands.

Robert May himself did not profit from the story at first. In fact, medical bills from his wife's terminal illness, and the six children he had to raise and support, made his Christmases anything but bright. In 1946, Montgomery Ward transferred the rights to May, who promptly sold the story to a children's book publisher. Over 100,000 copies of the book were sold during the 1947 and 1948 Christmas seasons. Then Johnny Marks, May's friend and brother-in-law, set the verse to music. Recorded by Gene Autry in 1949, it sold two million copies in its first season and ensured Rudolph's permanent fame. Over the next two decades, over 500 officially licensed Rudolph-related products appeared on store shelves, including everythingfrom slippers to lamps to cookie cutters and cuckoo clocks. May's book was published around the world in over two dozen languages, and in 1964 an animated Rudolph debuted as a Christmas television special.

CHRISTMAS CATALOGS

In a rural society, where large cities were few and far between and visits to town were once-a-week affairs, catalogs were an efficient way of exposing customers to merchandise and increasing sales by allowing them to place their orders by mail. In the the wake of World War II when paved roads and faster cars made town visits more common, the popularity of the catalog died off, right? Not at all. Anyone who was around in the 1950s and 1960s knows that catalogs were, if anything, even bigger than they'd been in the 1930s and 1940s.

Sears had long been the king of catalog retailers, having started as a mail-order company and only adding stores later on. Montgomery Ward and JC Penney also developed strong mail order businesses, focusing on customers in rural and small-town America. But as these chains expanded and more and more customers could, if

A
Fire Truck
16.95
or $3 monthly

B
All Steel
14.
or $3 m

Castelli

C
H
1
or $

HOT ROD

D
Deluxe Trike
17.95
or $3 monthly

E
Station
14
or $3

Town and Country
13.98
or $3 monthly

3-Wheel Scooter
1.98

Deluxe Scooter
3.98

TOWN AND COUNTRY

they chose, come into the store and see the merchandise for themselves, these "wish books," as they were nicknamed, remained important. Many customers preferred to browse the merchandise in the store but to make their actual buying decisions in the comfort of their homes. Suburban mothers who worked outside the home, ferried the kids to music lessons, led Brownie and Cub Scout groups, belonged to bridge clubs, took flower-arranging classes, and found time for a dozen other time-consuming activities their mothers had never dreamed of doing, found catalog shopping marvelously efficient. Not only could the modern woman accomplish a good deal of shopping in one swoop, she no longer had to drag a reluctant husband to the store — all she had to do was show him a picture and get a nod of approval.

The change in the way people used catalogs can be seen in the catalogs themselves. Where earlier catalogs had been full of practical and necessary items, catalogs published after World War II included a far greater range of gifts and luxury items, and in a far greater range of colors, fabrics, and styles. Mail-order counters became catalog departments, and even stores that didn't publish catalogs during the rest of year began sending Christmas catalogs to their customers.

Perhaps the key driving force behind the burgeoning Christmas catalog trade was the small customer — literally. It's hard to explain to anyone who wasn't around before 1965 the extent to which the world of the 1950s and 1960s seemed a world for and about children. The enormous number of babies born in the two decades after the Second World War created a seemingly limitless customer pool, and retailers were eager to get the little tykes' attention. The problem was how to do it. Children watched far less television in the 1950s than they did in any decade thereafter. Commercials for specific toys were less common and, due to fuzzy and fluttering reception and black-and-white technology, far less alluring. Before the arrival of local malls and super-

CREME DE LA CATALOG: THE NEIMAN-MARCUS CHRISTMAS BOOK

While most catalogs focused on moderately priced items, one catalog became famous for doing just the opposite. The first Neiman-Marcus catalog, sent in 1926, was an unexceptional 16-page booklet, but when Stanley Marcus, son of the store's co-founder, joined the firm, he decided to do something different. If store windows put the most glittering and most expensive items on display, why shouldn't a catalog do the same?

The idea garnered so much publicity that soon Marcus was going out of his way to dream up interesting and expensive gifts. In 1959, when backyard barbecuing was all the rage, the featured gift was a Black Angus steer accompanied by a silver-plated barbecue grill. In 1965, when the computer age was dawning, the Christmas Book's cover featured the Honeywell Kitchen Computer. At $10,600 it came with a two-week course in computer programming and was pre-loaded with recipes that had to be decoded before they could be put to use. His and Her luxury items were added in 1960, with twin Beechcraft airplanes going for just $149,000 and $127,000 respectively. Wealthy couples of 1962 could give each other matching Chinese junks, priced at $11,500 each. For ocean enthusiasts, there was 1963's two-person submarine, a bargain at $18,700. Far less costly were 1965's pink-striped hot air balloons, which sold for a mere $6,850 apiece.

Journalists found this particular kind of Christmas candy impossible to resist. Edward R. Murrow had his assistant, Walter Cronkite, call each year to find out what the expensive toy was to be, and Johnny Carson read descriptions on the Tonight Show. Soon the Christmas Book was an annual event.

stores, children spent less time in stores, and the time they did spend was more likely to be parent-supervised. Christmas catalogs, with page upon page of dolls, play forts, cowboy outfits, toy trains, and dollhouses, were the perfect solution. Mailed directly to the home, the phone book–sized, bursting-with-color catalog dropped into the child's lap well before shopping season began, giving mom and dad plenty of time to be begged to, pleaded with, and cajoled into buying the toys that glittered so temptingly. It's impossible to imagine how many catalogs were left open on dad's chair with certain items starred and circled, how many dinnertime conversations were filled with promises to be good, take out the garbage, wash the car, or make the bed every single day if only that one, magical toy would appear beneath the tree.

WOOLWORTH'S

Long before there were Kmart, Wal-Mart, and Target – all of which debuted in 1962 – there was Woolworth's. America's original discount store made a special effort at Christmas, never losing sight of the fact that part of the joy of the holiday was the sheer plentitude of it. Amidst a riotous jamboree of colors, lights, decorations, and gifts, signs welcomed customers to "America's Favorite Christmas Store." Woolworth's offered everything the big stores did but at scaled down prices, giving those who might otherwise have had a skimped Christmas the chance to have one that at least felt lavish. Parents could trim the tree and still fill stockings with chocolates and hard candies that sold for pennies a pound. Bright wrapping papers and ribbons could be had for a fraction of what they cost in tonier stores. Children discovered that, with a little careful planning, they could buy gifts with their very own money — a Tangee lipstick for sister, Evening in Paris perfume for mom, handkerchiefs or a new pipe for dad. And even after all that spending, there was still enough for a dish of ice cream at the lunch counter. Of course then, as now, not all bargain shoppers were those with slim wallets. Undoubtedly, there were plenty of customers who examined an item in the relaxing atmosphere of a department store, then bought it for less at Woolworth's, or who delighted in finding almost identical versions of brand name items they felt were over-priced. But whether one was bargain shopping for necessity, practicality, or the sheer fun of getting more for less, Woolworth's had something for all who entered.

Gifts for Grown-ups

Gifts have changed over the years, but our approach to giving them hasn't. A complex web of unspoken rules has almost always surrounded gift giving. For example, gifts you make yourself will be treasured if you're a grandparent or if you're exceptionally talented at something. Homemade candy is great for your neighbor or even your minister, but if you're a fashion designer, don't send it to the editor you want to feature your spring line. If you had a really good year, you could send your stock broker some homemade candy, but he should send you something swankier, like a desk diary or a charity donation in your name. And then there's the too-personal vs. not-personal-enough rule, which might make some handmade items desirable if the giver is very dear to the recipient, in which case the work needn't be completely top drawer, just heartfelt. You see the issues. It may be that women do most of the holiday shopping just because they're the only ones in full command of the nuances.

The average American family spends 4% of its annual income on gifts.

These basic rules haven't changed very much over time, just the items we slot into them. It is interesting to note how closely Christmas gifts reflect the era in which they are given. In hard times, people give gifts of practicality and everyday usefulness. But serious times, even if they are flush, yield practical and useful gifts too, just on a more luxurious level. When society goes through a mass movement — such as the space age of the late 1950s and early 1960s — people want to give and receive gifts that join them to the cultural shift. And when society goes haywire and scatters off in all directions, as it did in the late 1960s, you get Pet Rocks and mood rings. Here are some of the great gifts of the past, and what they say about where we've been.

WARTIME GIFTS

Ration stamps — which were nothing more than the permission to buy something at inflated prices — were one of the most appreciated gifts on the homefront. Practical and serviceable items like hats, mittens, wallets, socks, household and kitchen items were also popular. Home-canned and homegrown foods were frequently given — especially nuts, apparently, as there were many articles and recipes telling recipients how to use up the surplus. Sales of checkers, chess sets, and other simple games that could be played at home soared, as did book sales once publishers got around the paper shortage by inventing the paperback. Especially popular gifts for women were perfumes and cosmetics with patriotic names, such as Yankee Clover perfume and Victory Red lipstick. Men and boys enjoyed radios, atlases and magazine subscriptions that would allow them to follow the ever-changing front.

A WARTIME CHRISTMAS: WHAT THEY DID WITHOUT

Everyone's heard stories of mothers and grandmothers who drew seams up their legs to simulate no-longer-available nylon stockings, but it would take a master of imagination to think of even a fraction of the things people did without during World War II — or how it affected everything from daily bread to Christmas Day. Here are just a few of the things that weren't part of the holiday season.

Volleyballs, basketballs, tennis shoes, overshoes, hot water bottles, and just about anything else made with rubber, including new tires for the car.

New cars, typewriters, toy trains, pots and pans, strollers, tricycles, tin soldiers, alarm clocks, and other items made from metal, which was needed for airplanes, tanks, battleships, munitions, and equipment.

Driving to grandma's house or anywhere else that wasn't absolutely necessary. Americans not involved in vital war work could only purchase four gallons of gas per week, enough to drive about 60 miles. Later, this was reduced by a gallon.

New bicycles. Now a legitimate form of adult transportation, purchasing a new bike required a written certificate from the local ration board.

Department store and grocery store deliveries. If you bought it, it was usually up to you to figure out how to get it home.

Charge accounts. Bills had to be paid within two months or accounts were frozen. Buying on time, previously common, was sharply curtailed.

Long-distance calls. Civilians were urged to keep the lines free for soldiers.

Lavish Christmas parties. Even if you could get the food and the booze, you probably couldn't get anyone to prepare or serve it. Domestic help was in short supply unless you could match the wages paid by the war industry.

Being warm and cozy at home. As of 1942, homeowners could only purchase 66% of the heating oil they'd purchased in 1941. Theoretically, this allowed homes to be heated to 65° — but only theoretically. The winter of '42-'43 was unusually frigid, especially on the east coast. Eventually, firewood and coal were also rationed.

Their loved ones.

With the war over and many newly married couples trying to get their footing, gifts from husband to wife tended to be small-scale, with the real money going into savings for a big-ticket item like a house or a car. Labor-saving appliances were appreciated, especially by those who'd never had them before. A modest budget could spring for a vacuum cleaner (about $30), while more money to spend might mean a new electric washing machine (about $240). After the fabric sparing straight skirts of the war years, the Dior-inspired "New Look" dress, featuring full, ballet-length skirts, was high on any woman's list. After years in uniform, men had some wardrobe replenishing to do, too, and the new wide ties (part of what Esquire magazine described as the fresh, bold, and self-confident look for men) were also popular gift items.

The current fad, Canasta, made folding card-tables a popular gift of the era. Timex watches, which debuted in 1946, became one of the most popular gifts of the century by combining durable performance and a wide range of styles with relatively modest prices. For gadget lovers, the newly invented electric blanket seemed the ultimate in luxury living.

What did the really rich give each other? Well, for him there was a Rolls-Royce convertible, going for a mere $18,500 in 1948, and for her a mink from Bergdorf Goodman in New York, a bargain at $2,250.

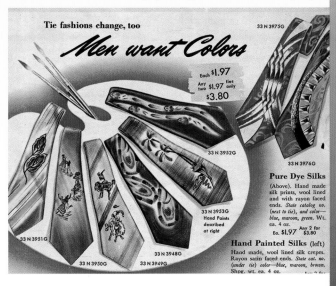

Tie fashions change, too

Men want Colors

33 N 3975G

Each **$1.97**

Any two **$1.97** ties only **$3.80**

33 N 3952G

33 N 3976G

Pure Dye Silks (Above). Hand made silk prints, wool lined and with rayon faced ends. State catalog no. (next to tie), and color—blue, maroon, green. Wt. ca. 4 oz.
Ea. $1.97 Any 2 for $3.80

33 N 3953G
Hand Paints described at right

33 N 3951G

Hand Painted Silks (left). Hand made, wool lined silk crepes. Rayon satin faced ends. State cat. no. (under tie) color—blue, maroon, brown. Shpg. wt. ca. 4 oz.

33 N 3950G   33 N 3949G   33 N 3948G

1940s SHOPPING LIST

* ❄ Folding card table, no chairs : $4

* ❄ Women's silk stockings, one pair: $1.49

* ❄ Women's full-length chenille robe with floral motiff: $4.98

* ❄ Copy of a Dior "New Look" dress in rayon: $20.

* ❄ Men's horsehide leather flight jacket: $21

* ❄ Sunbeam Shavemaster men's electric razor: $24.50

* ❄ Electric blanket, double bed: $28.95

* ❄ Table lamp: $8.95 - $12.50

* ❄ 45 rpm record, one song on each side: 25¢.

* ❄ Bing Crosby 78 rpm Christmas album: $3.95

* ❄ Portable record player: $15.95

GIFTS OF THE 1950s

The practicality and frugality of the war years persisted, partly out of long habit and partly because most people were either still saving for a home, trading to a larger one, or trying to furnish the place they'd finally managed to buy. During the 1950s, new housing starts ran into the millions — 1.5 million a year to be exact — each one in desperate need of sectional sofas, Barcaloungers, barstools, bunk beds, patio furniture, and washer-dryer combos. "Something for the house" became a popular Christmas gift for couples, and those with children frequently made it a gift the whole family could enjoy, such as a television set (black-and-white at first, then color) or a new rec room (referred to in those days as a rumpus room). Tools became a most-wanted gift for men of this era, many of whom had acquired an interest in and ability to operate all sorts of machines during their time with Uncle Sam. Women were self-reliant, too.

Many made their own curtains and sewed their own and their children's clothes, making a sewing machine one of the most popular gifts of the decade. Unlike portable machines of today, the sewing machine of the 1950s was a regal piece of furniture that came in its own polished wood cabinet and, when not in use, could pass as a living room side table.

During the second half of the decade, when spin-off technologies from the space race were putting new products on the shelves at ever more affordable price, gadgets and technology-oriented gifts became popular. Home movies were a popular fad throughout the decade. The first transistor radio came onto the market just before Christmas 1954. It was strictly a luxury item, selling at $49.95 for the radio, $3.95 for the leather case, and $7.50 for an

1950s SHOPPING LIST

※ Women's boots — $5

❋ Costume jewelry bracelet — $1.10

※ Women's gloves — $2

❋ Men's slipper socks — 70¢ - $2.98

※ Men's cuff links — $3.85

❋ Men's watch — $18

※ Reader's Digest subscription — $2.25

❋ Folding card table and chairs — $13.30

※ Bird cage — $3.50

❋ Portable LP record player — $47.80

※ Heppelwhite sewing machine cabinet with Sears Kenmore machine — $210

❋ 8mm movie camera and light bar — $55

※ 8mm movie projector and screen — $75

ELVIS THE GIVER

Elvis bought his beloved Graceland in the spring of 1957. His gift to his girlfriend, Anita Wood, that year was a poodle. His mother, Gladys, received a kitchen full of new appliances and a cashmere coat. During his last Christmas at Graceland, 1976, Elvis donated $1,000 to the local police station and an additional $52,000 to various charities. He gave several cars to friends and a few to strangers he'd never met.

earphone. To put things into perspective, that's $322, $25, and $48 respectively, in year 2000 values. Ouch! But for those who could wait, the prices dropped so rapidly that by the end of the decade you could get an 8-transistor model for about $9.

For many, a well-performing economy, low unemployment, and rising wages combined to make the first half of the 1960s a golden era. Members of the World War II generation were experiencing the first decade of uninterrupted peace and prosperity they'd ever know — and their backyards proved it. Patios, picnic tables, umbrella tables, and lawn furniture reflected the new attitude, as did the outdoor barbecue. Without a doubt, grilling equipment for dad was one of the most popular gifts of the era. Grills, electric starters, utensils large enough to handle a Flintstones-sized brontosaurus burger, hats and mitts and aprons — finally you knew exactly what to get dad. Another new fad was the built-in home bar, and the various styles of glasses, drink utensils, and other paraphernalia were also popular.

Fun loving Family? Picnics!

Dad, Mom, the children . . . all treasure the pleasure of a beautiful BARBECUE GRILL

$44⁹⁵ Cash
Only $4.50 Down on Easy Terms

New gadgets and appliances continued to be popular throughout the house. Mom threw her old coffee pot away the year she got one of the new "hostess-sized" electric ones, dad and his teenage offspring yearned for a jazzy hi-fi system. Many moms and daughters were thrilled to have one of the new, labor-saving automatic dishwashers. Just as the black-and-white television had been the #1 family gift of the 1950s, so a new color set was the must have of the early 1960s. Inexpensive portable sets were coming on the market, too, making it possible to have not one but several televisions throughout the house, and putting an end to innumerable pitched battles over what to watch. One of the most

"Victrola" 45 automatic table phonograph. 45EY2, $34.95

wished-for gifts of the century — at least by teenage girls — wasn't a new technology but a new style for it. After years of standard black desk telephones, the new Princess model was introduced. Not only was its streamlined oval shape instantly appealing, but it came in a variety of shades, including pink, turquoise, and cream. When one of Barbie's outfits included a phone as an accessory, millions of girls recognized a fashion trend in the making.

Many women went back to work, full- or part-time in the 1960s, and the first baby boomers were getting old enough to have driver's licenses. For the first time, middle-class families began to seriously think about acquiring a second car, and Christmas often seemed the perfect time to do it.

1960–65 SHOPPING LIST

❄ Electric coffee maker: $29.95

❄ Console hi-fi unit with speakers: $500

❄ 17" portable TV, black and white: $150

❄ Waring blender: $40

❄ Women's stretch pants: $13

❄ Volkswagon Beetle: $1695

❄ Cigarette case: $2

❄ Men's crew neck sweater: $12.95

❄ Brook's Brothers wool flannel blazer: $30

❄ Fly rod, reel, and lures: $50

SPIEGEL

85th
YEAR

Babes in Toyland

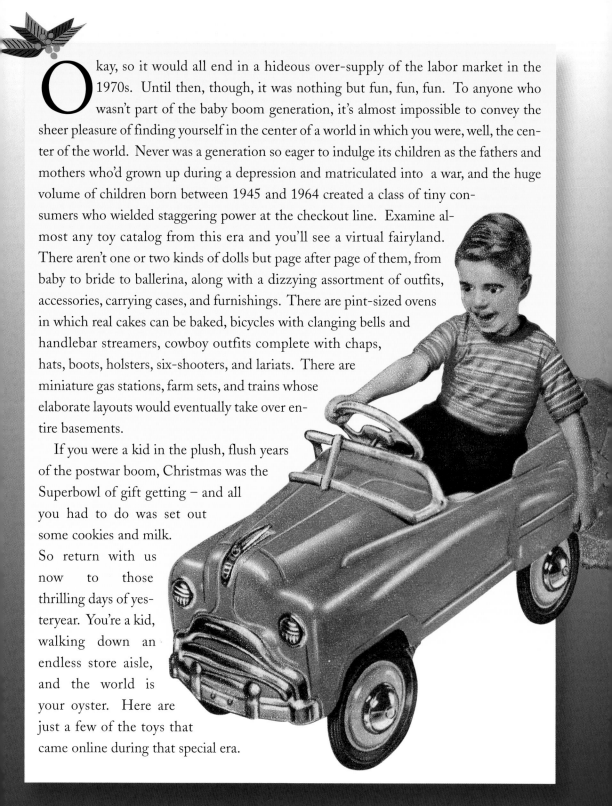

O kay, so it would all end in a hideous over-supply of the labor market in the 1970s. Until then, though, it was nothing but fun, fun, fun. To anyone who wasn't part of the baby boom generation, it's almost impossible to convey the sheer pleasure of finding yourself in the center of a world in which you were, well, the center of the world. Never was a generation so eager to indulge its children as the fathers and mothers who'd grown up during a depression and matriculated into a war, and the huge volume of children born between 1945 and 1964 created a class of tiny consumers who wielded staggering power at the checkout line. Examine almost any toy catalog from this era and you'll see a virtual fairyland. There aren't one or two kinds of dolls but page after page of them, from baby to bride to ballerina, along with a dizzying assortment of outfits, accessories, carrying cases, and furnishings. There are pint-sized ovens in which real cakes can be baked, bicycles with clanging bells and handlebar streamers, cowboy outfits complete with chaps, hats, boots, holsters, six-shooters, and lariats. There are miniature gas stations, farm sets, and trains whose elaborate layouts would eventually take over entire basements.

If you were a kid in the plush, flush years of the postwar boom, Christmas was the Superbowl of gift getting – and all you had to do was set out some cookies and milk. So return with us now to those thrilling days of yesteryear. You're a kid, walking down an endless store aisle, and the world is your oyster. Here are just a few of the toys that came online during that special era.

1942

❇ Little Golden Books publishes its first twelve titles: *The Three Little Kittens*, *Bedtime Stories*, *The Alphabet A-Z*, *Mother Goose*, *Prayers for Children*, *The Little Red Hen*, *Nursery Songs*, *The Pokey Little Puppy*, *The Golden Book of Fairy Tales*, *Baby's Book*, *The Animals of Farmer Jones* and *This Little Piggy*. One-and-a-half million copies are sold in the first five months alone.

❇ Forced to halt production in metal due to the war, toy manufacturer Lionel offers a paper train for the holiday season. In its *Model Builder* magazine and its *Railroad Planning Book*, the company urges boys and their dads to "plan your postwar railroad" now.

1943

❇ Chutes and Ladders, by Milton Bradley, creates a fervor among the four-to six-year-old set.

1945

❇ Slinky, the toy that can walk down stairs, is the novelty hit of the Christmas season. Its invention was a complete accident, and came about when marine engineer Richard James was considering using springs as antivibration devices.

1946

❇ With wartime shortages a thing of the past, Lionel returns to production. New products include locomotives that puff real smoke, remote-control coupling systems, and a water tower with a moveable spout. All aboooooard!

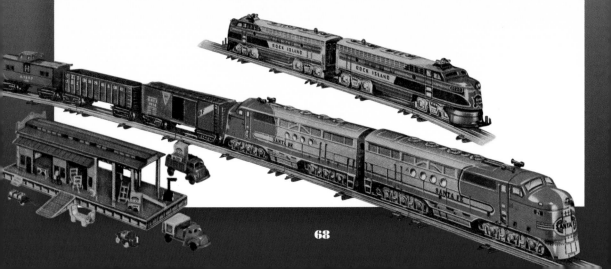

❄ The Wannatoy Coupe, with its Deco-style, bright plastic body, and clear plastic bubble top, is scarcely remembered today — but almost a million of them flew off the shelves during the 1946 Christmas season. Priced at just 25¢, kids could own one in every color.

1947

❄ From the shores of Gitchee Gumee — brightly colored, super-durable Tonka trucks are an instant hit with sandbox long-haulers. Early releases include Steam Shovel, Crane and Clam, and Lift Truck and Cart.

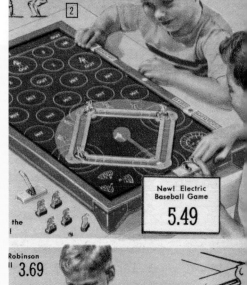

New! Electric Baseball Game
5.49

Robinson 3.69

"pitch" lever

❄ Ginny, an eight-inch doll made of hard plastic, is first produced by the Vogue Doll Company. Although Ginny has the same undeveloped, slightly pudgy shape that many of her owners do, her fashion sense is fully formed, and she is one of the first dolls to come with her own, separately sold line of clothing. Ginny retails for $1.98 wearing just shoes, socks, and panties, with the various outfits from her wardrobe retailing in the $1 to $2.98 range.

nothing else is
Silly Putty!
I take up comics—*in full color*
I stretch!
I Bounce
I make things!
BUY ME WHERE YOU BOUGHT THIS COMIC!
BUY ME WHEREVER TOYS ARE SOLD—

1949

❄ Crayon-manufacturer Binney & Smith raises the curtain on another hit — Silly Putty.

❄ Milton Bradley's Candyland debuts and becomes a top-selling board game.

❄ The board game Clue is marketed in America by Parker Brothers. We may have the culprit, but we still don't have a motive for Mr. Boddy's shocking murder.

❄ Roll the dice, be the first to assemble your multicolored bug, and you win. That was the idea behind the simple but wildly popular game of Cootie, from Schaper Toys. Who can forget the joyous cry of a young tot unwrapping his gift and crying "I got Cooties!" at the top of his lungs?

LATE 1940s–EARLY 1950s

❄ Plastic models become a fad with boys and their dads. The toys range from simple to complex and come in just about every form you can think of, from ships and cars to planes and military equipment. The fun is all in the assembly, since once the model is put together, it doesn't actually do anything. Some youngsters are so addicted they assemble a new model every week. Was it the fun of those tiny plastic bits or the heady scent of the glue?

❄ Although Lionel trains have been around for almost half a century, the early 1950s are a highwater mark, both in terms of popularity and in high-quality, innovative products. Lionel breaks the gender barrier with a pastel-hued Lady Lionel set just for girls, and looks toward the future by incorporating space age and Cold War themes into their trains. At one point, there are more engines and rolling stock in America's rec rooms than there are on actual railroads. For a few years, Lionel even has its own television show — an ironic note, since it's children's growing fascination with the tube that marks a waning of interest in toy trains.

❄ Dollhouses had been around for more than a century, but the invention of plastic created a revolution in doll house furniture. Hard plastic, durable and inexpensive, could be molded into highly detailed furnishings and appliances. Little girls

could furnish their miniature homes with tiny bureaus whose drawers actually opened, washing machines and dryers whose lids raised and lowered, telephones whose receivers could be lifted. Renwal, the hard-plastic toy company that would go on to manufacture Mr. Machine, even produced a sewing machine with a moving treadle and machine body that could be folded down into its cabinet.

❄ It's Howdy Doody time! America's favorite television marionette and his pals are so popular they create a mini toy storm as manufacturers rush to produce everything from marionettes and hand puppets to watches, board games, and cartoon "film" strips featuring Howdy, Buffalo Bob, Dilly-Dally, Mr. Bluster, Princess Summer-Fall-Winter-Spring, Clarabel the Clown, Zippy the Chimp, and everyone else in Doodyville.

1950

❄ Fisher-Price introduces the Buzzy Bee, a wooden pull-toy shaped like a bee whose yellow plastic wings not only rotated when pulled but made a delightful clacking sound. Further delight was added by red wooden balls that waved at the end of coiled-spring antennae.

❄ Hopalong Cassidy lunch boxes, inspired by the new TV hit, fly off the shelves. Before the year is out, over 600,000 have been sold.

A 36-key Spinet $23.69

B Toy Piano $3.19

C 8 Key Piano $1.98

D Phonograph $8.79

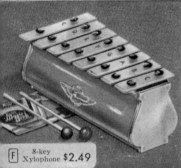

F 8-key Xylophone $2.49

G Toy Piano Key Accordion $2.98

H Toy Accordion $3.98

E Pho $1

L Twirl-a-Tune 89c

Farmer Dell

Christmas Favorites

Kiddie Favorites

1951

❄ Colorforms appear. While the first set is simple colored shapes, sets based on licensed characters — including Popeye, Bugs Bunny, and Walt Disney's Sleeping Beauty — follow in 1957.

1952

❄ Hasbro's Mr. Potato Head is the first toy advertised on television. Sales total $4 million in the first year alone.

❄ The Austrian candy, Pez, comes to America, just in time to stuff millions of stockings.

❄ The first Matchbox car, a miniature die-cast metal vehicle, is made. The first four models are a Road Roller, Massey Harris Tractor, Muir Hill Site Dumper, and Cement Mixer. More models of the wildly popular toys are added every year thereafter, and parents everywhere learn not to go into Junior's room barefoot.

Gumby has a sense of humor. He can laugh at himself.
— Art Clokely, Gumby's creator

1953

❄ Everybody's favorite toy boy, Gumby, hits the market. For Gumby, it was always easy being green — he and his horse, Pokey (who came along in 1955), had their own TV show from 1957 to 1964 and to this day the pair remain popular talismans for an entire generation. According to Art Clokely, inventor of the duo, hippies always "got" Gumby, and grooved on his inherent honesty.

❄ The Winky Dink Magic Television Screen, essential if you were to have any shot at enjoying the *Winky Dink Show*, was a popular Christmas item. By placing a bluish plastic screen over the TV and using magic crayons to trace briefly appearing lines, children ended up with a picture that became part of the story.

1954

❋ Ideal makes a lot of money out of gray plastic with Robert the Robot, a 14 inch nuts and bolts kind of a guy who walks (on cleverly concealed rollers) when buttons on a ray gun-shaped remote control are pressed. Cool!

1955

❋ The first lady in dolls, Madame Alexander, designs and markets Cissy, America's first full-figured, high-heeled doll.

❋ Fess Parker plays Davy Crockett on TV and American children acquire $100,000 worth of coonskin caps. So high is the demand that the racoon population is actually endangered.

COONSKIN CAP MANIA

❋ Maybe you think it happened when the Beatles came to America in 1964. Or at Woodstock in 1970. Nope. The first time the youth culture made their voices heard and created a marketing tsunami was considerably earlier. On December 15, 1954, Walt Disney aired the first of a three-part series, *Davy Crockett*, starring Fess Parker. Children who tuned in were thrilled with what they saw, and the folkloric story of the Alamo hero who was born on a mountain top in Tennessee fueled a nationwide mania.

Though the surprise hit aired too late to get merchandise out for Christmas 1954, the demand for all things Davy raged throughout the first half of 1955 and was revived when two more episodes were rushed into production and aired, shrewdly, in November and December. By the second Christmas, parents could choose from over 3,000 Crockett items. The theme song from the series alone sold over 10 million copies, and the demand for caps was so great the price of raccoon fur went from 25¢ a pound to $8.

By the end of the 1955 Christmas season, America's little b'ar killers were in possession of an estimated $100,000,000 worth of raccoon hats, costumes, clothes, moccasins, watches, wallets, tooth-

Authentic Hopalong Cassidy Outfits

brushes, lunch boxes, thermoses, tool kits, flashlights, cap guns, frontier rifles, powder horns, Alamo play sets, board games, puzzles, Tru Vu slides, ukeleles, rings and necklaces, story books, comic books, coloring and activity books, towels, rugs, bedspreads, and lamps. Grownups liked Davy too, apparently, as his likeness was also seen on telephones and, oddly, women's panties.

MID-1950S

❋ With Roy Rogers and Hopalong Cassidy going strong on Saturday mornings, it was only natural that cap guns became one of the most popular toys of the 1950s, for girls as well as boys. Gilded in bright, tooled-looking silver, they resembled the six-shooters of the Old West and came with holsters, gunbelts, and other realistic-looking accessories. Ah, the scent of spent caps wafting over suburbia!

"Smoky Joe" TWIN HOLSTER SET with Gold-Finish Guns

$4.98

A stand-out for looks, for value! Twin holsters in black leather, with white pockets. Decorated with name "Smoky Joe" in gilt letters, jewels and nickel spots. Leather belt has four dummy bullets, jeweled rosettes and Western style buckle. Two gold-finished "Smoky Joe" repeater cap pistols shoot smoke with regular roll caps.

1956

✳ Uncle Milton's Ant Farms are marketed, much to the horror of mothers everywhere.

✳ Play-Doh comes on the market. Originally available only in off-white, a three-pack containing red, blue, and yellow is sold the next year. In 1957, white is brought back to make the classic four pack.

✳ Once upon a time, a wealthy couple from Canada invented a game to play on their boat. Whenever friends came aboard, they begged to play the "yacht" game. The couple sold the rights, and the game, Yahtzee, made its debut in 1956. It wasn't a hit, however, until the manufacturer started throwing Yahtzee parties so that people could discover just how much fun the game was to play.

1957

✳ Wham-O's Frisbee whirls onto the scene. Can hippies and dogs in red bandanas be far behind?

✳ Prehistoric Times play sets, by Marx, offer kids a chance to enter a world in which cavemen fought dinosaurs, prehistoric mammals, and all manner of extinct predators for conquest of the Earth. At just $5 for a 47-piece set, it was the buy of the season.

1958

✳ Wham-O scores big again, this time with the Hula Hoop. Over 25 million of the colored plastic loops are sold in the first two months.

❄ Although do-it-yourself kids have been nailing boards to roller skates since the 1930s, the skateboard finally becomes a manufactured item. Thousands of dads, trying to prove they're still hip, end up with sprains and bruises.

1959

❄ Fisher-Price markets the Safety School Bus, introducing their Little People to ours.

❄ Kenner's Give-a-Show Projector is a Christmas season sell-out. Instead of being embarrassed by dad's slides of last summer's vacation, kids could give their own shows. The projector came with slide strips featuring popular figures from TV like Popeye, Yogi Bear, Huckleberry Hound, the Three Stooges, and Wild Bill Hickock.

❄ Mattel's Barbie catwalks onto the shelves and millions of young girls start learning how to accessorize. For years, toymakers and sociologists alike insisted that little girls like "child" dolls that allowed them to play Mom. Barbie creator Ruth Handler had a different idea. Why not make a doll that let girls pretend they were grown-up teenagers? Handler was right and Barbie, the teenage fashion model, has been a best-seller since her debut at the New York Toy Fair. The original Barbie was a pony-tailed blonde who came in a black-and-white striped strapless swimsuit and sold for $3. A dazzling variety of sold-separately outfits — each with meticulously detailed accessories – allowed her to be ready for everything from slumber parties to singing in a nightclub. Since being blonde and beautiful means you never have to be alone for long, Barbie was joined by boyfriend Ken in 1961, best friend Midge in 1963, and little sister Skipper in 1964. Yeah, yeah, we know, if Barbie were real, her measurements would be 39"-18"-33", but she isn't, so there.

1960

❄ Mattel creates Chatty Cathy, the first talking doll. Her voice was supplied by June Foray, who was also the voice of Rocky the Flying Squirrel from *Rocky and Bullwinkle*.

❄ The game of Life, by Milton Bradley, prepares millions of baby boomers for adult milestones like love and marriage; as well as unemployment, debt, and bankruptcy.

❄ The first Etch-a-Sketch is sold. If you didn't get one, don't worry — they're still being made by the original manufacturer, Ohio Art.

✳ One of the most popular educational toys of all time arrives from Renwal. The Visible Man is a realistic model human whose three-dimensional organs are visible through his clear plastic skin. The Visible Woman follows close behind. Like her counterpart, her organs can be taken out and examined by curious little premeds. Go on, see if you can get 'em all back in there.

1961

✳ Ideal's Mr. Machine is the high-tech toy of the season. Bright red, 18 inches tall, with a bright blue wind-up key and colored gears you could see turning as he walked, the grinning robot broke barriers by appealing to girls as well as boys.

1962

✳ Legos, the Danish building bricks, are sold in the United States for the first time. In Danish, *lego* means "play well."

✳ Sea Monkeys become the trendy — if weird — stocking stuffer of the year. Marketed since 1960 in 49¢ packages labeled "Instant Life," the product didn't take off until an aggressive marketing campaign renamed them and emphasized their ability to learn tricks, race each other, and generally astound their owners. So what were Sea Monkeys? Tiny brine shrimp that could exist in a dehydrated state for long periods of time but come miraculously back to life when rehydrated.

✳ It's the debut of Tammy, Ideal's entry in the fashionista doll derby. Think of her as Barbie's wholesome sister, the one who wears kitten heels and is on the cheerleading squad. Unsurprisingly, mothers far prefer her to Barbie. Equally unsurprisingly, their daughters don't.

1963

✳ Mousetrap, by Ideal, initiates a trend in play action board games.

✳ Whoever thought cake made over a 100-watt bulb would taste this good? Kenner's Easy-Bake Oven, in stylish turquoise, offers little girls a chance to cook "just like mom" for $15.95. Small foil packets of cake, brownie, and cookie mix are included, along with a cook book for the more adventurous gourmet. Around this same time, Julia Child's *French Chef* debuts on television. Surely this is more than mere coincidence.

VALUE

⑥ Outfit $2.88

⑪ Outfit $2.88

② Outfit $2.98

G.I. JOE

AS SEEN ON TV .. the Best Equipped Fighting Man Ever!

Boys! America's Movable Fighting Men. Collect them all in basic uniforms—Air Force, Navy, Marine and Army—(1), (5), (10) and (16) below. At the same time, add the outfits . . scaled reproductions of actual uniforms and equipment.

Each G.I. Joe is of durable vinyl plastic, abt.

12 inches tall . . has 21 movable parts. Assumes all the action poses of a rugged military man . . charging, running, firing, throwing grenades. **Training Manual Included** for the particular branch of the service. Tells about all phases of military life and how to use equipment and gear.

⑰ Outfit $1.29

① **G.I. Joe Action Pilot** in fatigues, cap, jump boots, dog tags, insignia.
48 T 2793—Wt. 1 lb. **$1.98**

② **Air Force Flight Suit,** air vest, pistol, helmet, flightboard and belt.
48 T 2796—Wt. 1 lb. . **$2.98**

③ **Air Force Dress Uniform;** wings, Captain's bars.
48 T 2795—Wt. 13 oz. **$2.98**

④ **AF Life Raft** with flare gun, vest, anchor.
48 T 2794—Wt. 12 oz. **$2.29**

⑤ **G.I. Joe Action Sailor** in work uniform, dog tags, insignia.
48 T 2787—Ship. wt. 1 lb.....**$1.98**

⑥ **Navy Shore Patrol Outfit.**
48 T 2792—Ship. wt. 1 lb. **$2.88**

⑦ **Navy Scuba Suit** with tanks, fins, mask, depth gauge, knife and scabbard and "dynamite."
48 T 2790—Ship. wt. 15 oz. . **$3.49**

⑧ **Navy Life Raft Set.**
48 T 2789—Ship. wt. 12 oz. **$1.98**

⑨ **Navy Life Preserver Set.**
48 T 2791—Ship. wt. 12 oz. **$1.98**

⑩ **G.I. Joe Action Marine** in fatigues, boots, cap, dog tags, and insignia.
48 T 2747—Ship. wt. 1 lb.........**$1.98**

⑪ **Marine Dress Uniform,** pistol and rifle.
48 T 2750—Ship. wt. 13 oz......**$2.88**

⑫ **Marine Paratrooper Set,** accessories.
48 T 2749—Ship. wt. 13 oz......**$2.49**

⑬ **Marine Beachhead Field Pack Set.**
48 T 2785—Ship. wt. 1 lb.......**$3.29**

⑭ **Marine Beachhead Tent Set.**
48 T 2784—Ship. wt. 1 lb. **$2.98**

⑮ **Marine Communications Post Poncho Set.**
48 T 2748—Ship. wt. 15 oz......**$2.79**

⑯ **G.I. Joe Action Soldier** in fatigue uniform
48 T 2740—Ship. wt. 1 lb..............

⑰ **Army Field Jacket,** helmet, rifle and belt.
48 T 2741—Ship. wt. 8 oz..............

⑱ **Army Pup Tent Set,** netting, foliage, etc.
48 T 2744—Ship. wt. 12 oz..............

⑲ **Army Sleeping Bag,** rifle, mess kit, etc.
48 T 2743—Ship. wt. 13 oz..............

⑳ **Army Communications Set.** Poncho, radio
48 T 2745—Ship. wt. 1 lb..............

㉑ **Army Military Police Uniform,** accessories
48 T 2746—Ship. wt. 15 oz..............

㉒ **Army Field Pack,** mess kit, canteen, etc.
48 T 2742—Ship. wt. 1 lb..............

AIR FORCE

① ③ ④

NAVY

⑦ ⑤ ⑧ ⑨

⑫ MARINE ⑩ ⑬ ⑭ ⑮

ARMY

⑱ ⑯ ⑲ ⑳ ㉑

1964

❄ Troll dolls become a source of whimsey and good luck. Introduced for children, the small, rubbery dolls catch on with adults. Even the President's wife, Lady Bird Johnson, admits to owning one. By the end of the decade, trolls are the second best-selling doll in America. Who says looks are everything?

1965

❄ Wham-O manufactures the high-bouncing Super Ball. Between its summer debut and Christmastime, over seven million balls are sold. Suggested retail price: 98¢.

❄ G.I. Joe is the surprise hit of the toy season. Joe's female counterpart, brought out a few years later, is a complete flop.

❄ Creepy Crawlers becomes to boys what the Easy-Bake Oven is to girls. By squirting billious-colored Plastigoop into the heated molds of the Thingmaker, you could make giant bugs, worms, and monsters. You could also burn and cut yourself, not to mention create a permanent bond between spilled Plastigoop and mom's carpet. Fun!

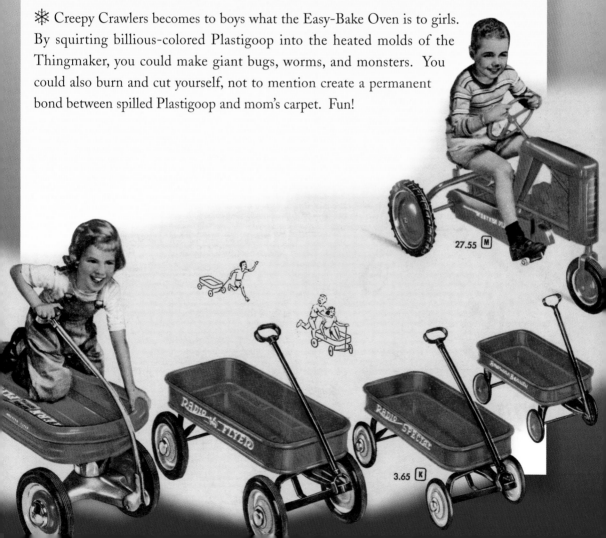

A Thoroughly
Modern Santa

You know him as the big guy in the red, red suit. Ten-league boots of shiny black. Cheeks like polished apples. He's the go-to guy for big-ticket toys, a jolly superhuman totally devoted to making every childhood a happy one. He's the one and only Santa, now and forever. This is the Santa you know, the modern Santa. His Santa forebearers were neither fat nor jolly. They didn't necessarily wear red and they didn't go barreling through the sky in toy-laden sleighs. There was no Mrs. Claus and certainly no elves.

Early Santa was a saint. Literally. The real Nicholas, a bishop who lived in the fourth century, gave food and gifts to the poor anonymously, leaving them outside their doors at night and filling the stockings of poor young girls with dowries of golden coins. His fame for these good deeds spread across Europe, earning him sainthood and mythic status. Many feel that because St. Nicholas died in December, he inevitably became associated with Christmas. It became popular in Europe to portray St. Nicholas as a thin old gentleman dressed in robes, traveling the snowy landscape on foot to deliver food and gifts to the poor at yuletide, sometimes carrying a pack upon his bent back and sometimes accompanied by a bear laden with packs. While children appreciated the goodies left in their shoes or stockings, this was not the kind of Santa whose lap who wanted to sit in.

THE AMERICAN CLAUS — FROM THIN AND DOUR TO FAT AND HAPPY

Santa began his transition from wispy spirit to cheerful fat man in 19th-century America. Clement Moore's famous poem described him as a "right jolly old elf" and made it clear that his obligation wasn't to the poor but to children. He no longer distributed necessary items like food and clothing but handed out luxurious toys — dolls that said "Mama," elaborate sets of toy soldiers,

A $29.95 *Without Battery* Holly green, Burgundy, Glacier gray, Sandalwood tan

B $22.95 *Without Battery* Holly green, Burgundy, Glacier gray

C $14.95 *Without Battery* Sea green

miniature tea sets and bicycles too big to wrap. Mom and dad could be counted on for a few toys, for books and clothing and other modest items, but in a growing number of households it was Santa who left the really coveted goods.

Still, the actual image of Santa remained somewhat hazy. Although Moore's poem added plumpness, giving him a stomach that "shook like a bowl full of jelly," his height was indeterminate. There was no mention of his clothing and, when asked to draw him, Moore's own daughter dressed him in green. Though Santa was becoming more child-friendly, he was still more of an idea than an actual man.

I stopped believing in Santa Claus when my mother took me to see him in a department store, and he asked for my autograph.
— **Shirley Temple**

This began to change in the 1930s, when magazines boomed and radio gave millions of Americans common cultural reference points. Santa appeared in hundreds of Christmas stories and his voice was heard over the airwaves. He became so interwoven with the day-to-day fabric of life that people expected not only to hear him and read about him but to see him as well. Store owners were the first to respond, hiring Santas to greet customers and listen to children's wish lists. The first school for Santas opened in the late 1930s. For $150, students received a week- long course in salesmanship, showmanship, toys, and child psychology. A union — the National Association of Professional Santas — was formed soon afterward. Although the work was seasonal, a professional Santa could expect to earn about $75 a week, approximately three times the average weekly wage.

Advertisers were quick to follow the stores' success, using Santa's image to boost holiday sales. By 1938, researchers noted that over 20% of ads in popular magazines like *Ladies Home Journal* and *The Saturday Evening Post* used Santa to sell one product or another. An article titled "The Santa Claus Industry," appearing in *The American Mercury* in 1940, lamented the fact that the beloved childhood icon had "gone completely commercial." Santa had became a super-salesman, credited with moving millions of dollars worth of merchandise a year.

RUSSIAN MISSILE OR INCOMING SANTA?

Almost from the start, Santa had served as an informal member of the military. During World War II and the Korean War he appeared at hundreds of far-from-home Christmas parties and USO shows. Illustrators showed him flying his reindeer in a V-for-victory formation and leaving bomb-shaped gifts in the stockings of America's enemies. And during the Cold War, Santa's annual flight was one of the few fun aspects of the scary new atomic age. It started in 1955 with a department store ad in a Colorado Springs newspaper that included the number of the store's special Santa line. The number had a one-digit typo, and when children dialed it, they were connected with the Operations Hotline of the Continental Air Defense Command, the agency in charge of detecting incoming enemy missiles. On the other end of the line was Colonel Harry Shoup, who quickly figured out what had happened and played along. Claiming to be one of Santa's helpers, Shoup explained that his job was to keep the skies safe

for Santa's journey, and told the excited children that he could see Slanta's sleigh on the radar monitor in front of him.

The story was picked up by the media, and the next year children purposely called the number, requesting a Santa update. By the time the Continental Air Defense Command became the North American Aerospace Defense Command (NORAD) in 1957, "Santa tracking" had become a new tradition. For children across the country, there was an inevitable thrill when Christmas Eve broadcasters interrupted normal programming to report an unidentified incoming object. Was it a nuclear attack? Was it time to duck and cover ? The split-second shiver of fear made the report of Santa's progress all the more fun. Little toes uncurled and little hearts started beating again, relieved and happy to learn that the nuclear bullet had been dodged one more time, allowing Christmas to go forward as usual.

Let's Get Together

The tradition of gathering with friends and family over the holiday season is as old as Christmas itself, but the ways in which we get together are always changing. We no longer, for example, storm the local baron's castle and demand to be wined and dined. Nor do we look forward, as medieval folks did, to troops of mimes dropping by to act out the Christmas story. Even some of the practices below have already undergone changes. Here's a look back.

GETTING THERE

For the first part of the 20th century, getting together with family and close friends over the holidays usually meant driving, or even walking, a fairly short distance. Then World War II came and set America on a course of perpetual motion from which it has yet to recover. It wasn't just that servicemen and women were shipped overseas, they were also shipped to dozens of camps and bases around America. Civilians were on the move too, as thousands of them left farms and small towns to find work in defense plants that were operating all day, everyday. If you had more than a few miles to go to

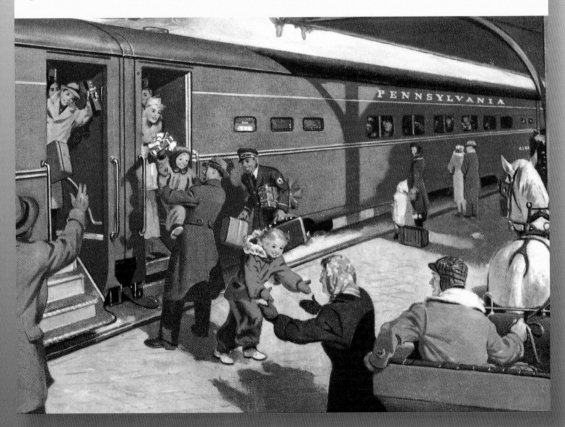

spend Christmas with your loved ones during the war, good luck. Gas rationing and shortages ruled out travel by auto, steamships had been converted to battleships, express buses had been discontinued, and priority status was required to get an airplane ticket. This left everyone competing for the two remaining forms of mass transit – trains and non-express buses. Lines at train windows were endless, prices almost invariably inflated by mysterious "surcharges" and add-ons, and even if you got a ticket, it was bound to be for a pullman car. The only way to get sleeping accommodations was to buy a ticket from Mr. Black, the slang term for shady black marketeers. As for buses, passengers waited for hours, only to discover, when it finally arrived, that the vehicle was too crowded to take on a single additional passenger.

After the war, travel became possible once more. Gas rationing ended and shiny new automobiles again rolled off the assembly lines. To facilitate a nation on the go, the Eisenhower administration initiated construction of an interstate highway system, allowing drivers to get from Point A to Point B far more rapidly than before. Although normal plane travel resumed after the war, it remained something of a luxury. To fly a family of four to grandma's house would have been a big deal indeed, something that most people would consider a special treat rather than an annual pilgrimage. For the most part, people drove or took the bus or train. But mostly, they drove, and hardly a traveler from this era doesn't have at least one memory of being stranded in a blizzard or turning back when the roads became too hazardous.

FANCY DRESS

Once you got where you were going, or once your guests got to you, it was important to be dressed in your best. After the poverty of the Depression and the fabric shortages of the war, Americans got into the idea of dressing for the holidays with gusto. A

new shirt, blouse, or dress was practically mandatory, and there were often new caps, scarves, shoes, and jewelry as well. Clothes often reflected the holiday theme, as can be seen in family pictures of dads in red vests, brothers in reindeer-strewn sweaters, mom in green velvet, and little girls in angelic blue.

DRESSING THE PART

1949: Santa's Helper reindeer slipper socks — $2.79

1951: Frosty the Snowman rayon scarf, 24" x 24" — 98¢

1957: Men's pullover sweater with skier or reindeer — $7.95

1960: Boy's red knit polo shirt — $2.50

1965: Christmas corsage — 70¢

During the 1950s and 1960s matching outfits became especially popular for families. You might see dad and the boys dressed in white shirts and red bow ties, and sisters (or sisters plus mom) in full-skirted look-alike dresses. Over the years, a whole industry grew up around Christmas-themed accessories — stockings patterned with Christmas trees, aprons decorated with holly and poinsettias, earrings dangling with tiny Christmas balls, and Christmas corsages that ran the gamut from reasonably tasteful snow-frosted ribbons and bells to plastic Santas with light-up noses.

PARTIES AT HOME

In the 1950s and 1960s the most common types of gatherings were cocktail parties and informal dinners. It was the Great Age of the Chafing Dish, and women's magazines were full of tips on how to be the perfect hostess. Christmas is still party time, but the volume of at-home parties doesn't seem quite as high as it was then. It may not be that we're less social, just that our customs have changed. In the United States today, the two days of the year on which the most parties are thrown are New Year's Eve and Super Bowl Sunday.

Many decried the drinking that went on at cocktail parties, and feared the hard edges of modern life would ruin "traditional" Christmases forever. In fact, the custom of knocking back a few started long before the 1950s. The Puritans also felt Christmas had

been turned into a sham, and Cotton Mather protested the drinking, dancing, and profligate merry-making that came with the season. He had a point — birth rates in Colonial America show a predictable rise nine months after each holiday season.

The punch bowl glistens, conversation sparkles, and your buffet party succeeds! Serve crisp cheese wafers, potato chips, and peanut butter dip.

— *Ladies Home Journal*, December, 1952

HANG A SHINING STAR UPON THE HIGHEST BOSS: THE OFFICE PARTY

In Dickens's *A Christmas Carol*, Scrooge's one-time boss, Mr. Fezziwig, thanks his employees for their labors with a jolly Christmas party. There was fiddle music and dancing yet, despite the presence of a brimming punch bowl, everyone behaved themselves. There were no reports of clerks caught with their sleeve garters down, and no wives coming to drag husbands home by the ear. Fast forward a hundred years and you'll find the boss draped over a desk and half the typing pool doing a can-can around him.

What happened?

The custom of employer-employee festivities dates all the way back to feudal times, when wealthy lords were obliged to welcome peasants into their homes. Food and drink in abundance — something most medieval people had access to only a few times in their lives — were the centerpiece of these celebrations. In the modern version, food became a handful of cocktail peanuts and drink expanded to fill whole water coolers.

By the 1950s and early 1960s, so many office parties had become such bacchanalian affairs that magazines addressed them as a serious social threat. In the December 1947 issue of *Ladies Home Journal*, it was the featured topic of their regular "Can This Marriage Be

Saved?" column. "Looking back over some 30,000 unhappy marriages with which we have dealt in the American Institute of Family Relations," wrote counselor Paul Popenoe, "it is interesting to remember how many of them have been worsened by a Christmas party at the office." The article is largely his-and-her tales of lament — his of his wife's failure to understand that attendance is required of up-and-coming young executives, hers of her husband's choice to "mingle socially with a lot of man-crazy young subordinates."

How the mid-century office party got so out-of-hand is a matter of speculation. Many note that, after the privations of Prohibition and the war, the 1950s was one long cocktail party. Yet alcohol consumption was not really that different from what it had been in other decades. The unbridled merriment might also be seen as having been an escape valve for a generation of men in gray flannel suits. But perhaps the most significant fact was the one identified by Elsa, the young wife in the *Journal* story — a combustible combination of mostly married male executives and young, mostly unmarried female subordinates. Or is it sheer coincidence that, with the dawning of the women's movement and the increasing numbers of career women in the workplace, the office party of old faded like last year's tinsel?

CHRISTMAS EVE OR CHRISTMAS DAY?

It's one of those questions that must be asked before marrying someone, as important as "How many kids should we have?" and "City apartment or country house?" — Do you do Christmas on Christmas Eve or Christmas Day? To be sure, most people do something on both, but what people do on each of these days can differ radically. For some people, Christmas Eve is the big event, with friends and family gathering together for a festive smorgasbord, while Christmas Day is spent quietly at home, with just the nuclear family. In other homes, Christmas Eve is the quiet time, and Chistmas Day the time for visiting and hoopla. The same variations that apply today applied forty, fifty, and sixty years ago, although the spectrum of options was somewhat narrower. The idea of going to a movie on Christmas Day, for example, would have struck most people as hopelessly secular, and even going to a Christmas Eve concert would have seemed avant garde. If the TV went on, it was probably in the home of some lone Scrooge, or to let dad enjoy a few soothing minutes of Johnny Carson while he

struggled with Santa's easy-to-assemble toys. Without computers, video games, or DVDs to rely on, most parents of this era developed inventive strategies to distract children during the last few hours before the wrapping paper came off. Some families went to candlelight church services, some drove around and looked at houses and yards decorated with lights, some sent the kids off to the local ice rink for the afternoon. So great was the pressure that many parents broke Christmas into a two-part event regardless of how they themselves had been raised, allowing some presents to be opened on Christmas Eve, and saving Santa's gifts for Christmas Day.

Eat Till It Hurts

Few traditions are more time-honored than that of holiday feasting. In Europe, December was the about the only time of year when meat could be slaughtered and enjoyed fresh, without fear of spoilage or need for salt curing. The abundance of fresh protein dovetailed nicely with the holiday, and society's less well off — who outnumbered the well off by a huge margin — turned events to their advantage by emphasizing the obligation of the haves to give to the have-nots. Christmas became a time when the normal social order was turned on its head. Tenants and peasants could knock on their landlords' doors and be granted welcome. Once inside, it was up to the lords and ladies of the manor to feed them and provide beverage. Sometimes the guests sang for their suppers (the origins of caroling), sometimes they did not. The whole tradition worked a bit like trick or treating, and woe to the lord who provided scraps or meager fare. Today, despite the fact that many of us are all too adequately fed to begin with, we still equate the holiday season with feeding ourselves and our guests better-than-everyday fare.

WORLD WAR II FARE

Christmas dinners just weren't the same during the war. For military personnel, nothing could make up for the glumness of being away from home. The government did its best, however. While non-perishables like canned meat and vegetables, dehydrated fruit, and powdered eggs made up the bulk of military fare at other times, Uncle Sam went to extraordinary lengths to provide fresh meats at Christmas and Thanksgiving. Even families that could be together on the homefront found that rationing cut into what, and how much, was available. For example, individuals were entitled to no more than 28 ounces of meat, four ounces of cheese, four ounces of butter, and half a pound of canned vegetables per week. Sugar shortages challenged candy-makers and bakers alike. There was even a black market in bubble gum — and the fence was usually a 10-year-old. You could forget the eggnog as well, since not only were milk and butter rationed, but the high cost of feed and labor drove many dairy farmers out of business. By 1944, real liquor had virtually disappeared, bringing back the bad old days of bootlegging. Eggs, however, were plentiful, so if you could devise a nonalcoholic dairy free eggnog, you'd be in business.

POST-WAR PLENTY

After the war, things didn't just return to normal, they boomed. In addition to a cessation of shortages and relatively moderate prices, whole new kinds of foods were available. The strides made in shelf-stable packaging during the war turned into civilian treats like boxed cake mixes and instant pudding, and frozen foods — especially vegetables — began to make harvest-style eating a year round possibility. So great was the sense of plenty, and the gratitude for it, that a favorite centerpiece of the mid-1950s was the cornucopia, spilling apples and grapes, tangerines and nuts down the length of the Christmas table.

Because so many people had been exposed to the flavors of Europe, Japan, the Phillippines and Korea, menus became more varied as well. Before the later 1940s, one seldom sees references to any other entrée but turkey being served on Christmas Day. Afterwards, magazines begin offering recipes for alternative meals such as ham, prime rib and lamb.

THAT FAMOUS CASSEROLE

After 1955, the holiday eating season would never be the same. That was the year one of America's most famous dishes, Green Bean Casserole, was introduced to the public. The recipe was published by the Campbell Soup Company as a way of promoting use of its cream soups in cooking. But the ingredient that became famous wasn't a Campbell's product at all. It was Durkee's French Fried Onions, known

today as French's Fried Onions. Canned, crunchy, and — let's face it — pretty darned tasty, the onions were regarded as a somewhat exotic ingredient that made an ordinary recipe something special. The dish became an instant tradition in millions of homes, possibly because it affords the cook an opportunity to snack on a few of the batter-fried tidbits as a reward for hours of holiday cooking. The Green Bean Casserole tradition continues to this day. According to the French's company, 50% of all French Fried Onion consumption occurs on just three days — Thanksgiving, Christmas, and Easter Sunday.

HAVE A HANDFUL!

Another 1955 recipe had an equally long-lasting effect. Chex cereals, perhaps in an effort to make it's products better withstand the onslaught of new, kid-popular cereals like Sugar Pops and Trix, introduced a recipe for Party Mix. Combining Wheat, Corn, and Rice Chex with nuts and pretzels and a dressing of melted butter, Worcestershire sauce, and onion and garlic powder, Chex Party Mix was the snack hit of the 1955 holiday season, and many seasons thereafter.

CHRISTMAS COOKIES

Glistening sugar and colored icing, red and green sprinkles and silver dragees, cutters in the shape of bells, bows, reindeer, and toys — by the middle of the 20th century, the decorated cutout cookie had become *the* holiday pastry, replacing all the stollens, plum puddings, bûches de Noëls and julekakas favored by America's immigrant ancestors. The shaped cookie cutter stamping out cookies in festive shapes is the American take on a tradition that dates back to medieval Europe, when monks began making molded gingerbread-like pastries to sell at holiday festivals. The cookie cutter was born in America, the invention of Pennsylvania Dutch tinsmiths who devised them as an affordable alternative to expensive, hand-carved cookie molds. With the first crude star or Santa, the American style Christmas cookie was born. People who grew up in the 1940s and early 1950s may remember a few

brief years when cutters were made not of metal but of clear red plastic. Although we haven't been able to pinpoint the year these cutters were first made, a likely theory is that they appeared during World War II, when tin was needed for the war effort. Though beautiful to look at, the cutters lacked the sharp cutting edge of their metal counterparts, and the rigid plastic could crack and break. After the war, with aluminum and other metals again in abundance, the metal cookie cutter returned.

The wartime metal shortage may also have prompted the proliferation of other types of holiday cookies. Though the drop cookie was certainly not new, Christmas-themed drop cookies — with names like Santa's

Whiskers, Ribbon Cookies, and Stained Glass Windows — began replacing rolled cookies as the most frequently made treats in the postwar era. Throughout the 1950s and 1960s, new varieties were added at a staggering clip, and the annual holiday cookie section became a major feature in magazines like *Better Homes and Gardens*, *McCall's*, *Good Housekeeping*, and *Woman's Day*.

Ten percent of American households leave milk and cookies for Santa Claus on Christmas Eve.

In the gadget-loving 1950s, spritz cookies also became extremely popular. Why go to all the trouble of rolling, frosting, and decorating cookies when you could tint some dough, squeeze Christmas trees and wreaths out of your new cookie press, and dust with the colored sugar crystals that were now available in grocery stores? Even quicker were cookies that required no baking at all. Kellogg's had scored a huge hit in the 1940s by introducing a recipe for Rice Krispie Treats, and home cooks started looking around for other unlikely food combinations. By the late 1950s, cornflakes mixed with melted chocolate and spooned into clusters, as well as chow mein noodle haystacks held together by melted butterscotch morsels, were extremely popular.

No one kitchen could possibly turn out all these varieties, so it was only natural that a shortcut be found. Holiday cookie exchanges quickly became an annual event in suburban America. Each woman in the group would make one or two types of cookies in large quantities, bundle them up in Tupperware, and show up at the hostess's house at the appointed hour. Cookies would be arranged buffet style, coffee would be sipped, and a good deal of sampling would take place while each woman refilled her brand new Tupperware with a variety of cookies baked by her friends. For kids in the burbs, it was a big deal when mom came home with the haul.

LOOKS GOOD...TASTES EVEN BETTER!

Jane Parker FRUIT CA[KE]

Traditional
AMERICAN TREAT

Made from a treasured old recipe

The rich, hearty flavor of Jane Parker Fruit Cake is your
proof that it's made with extra-fine ingredients.
Each pound of this luscious fruit cake
contains over 60% of fruits and nuts—
plump, juicy raisins, tangy citron and orange peel,
glazed pineapple and cherries, meaty, crunchy,
pecans. Be sure to get your Jane Parker Fruit
Cake early this year, as the supply is limited.
You'll be pleasantly surprised by its low
price—delighted by its quality.

A&P

PIES AND CAKES

Other than Victorian holdovers like fruit cake and mince pie, we don't think of pies and cakes as Christmas fare, despite recurrent efforts of vendors of those products to make it otherwise. That said, there's one pie — scarcely heard of today, much less eaten — that's invariably associated with this era. During the 1940s, a New York baker named Hortense Spier did a brisk business selling her pies to local restaurants. One of her specialties, Nesselrode pie, proved so popular it was soon copied by professional and home bakers alike. It became particularly associated with Christmas because of its basic ingredient — candied fruit and sweet chestnuts in a creme filling.

CHRISTMAS CANDY

Candy has always been an important part of the holiday scene. It's for the children, of course — but as far as we can tell, adults get their fair share as well. The first "store bought" Christmas treats included candy canes and, for those who could afford them, more expensive and colorful choices. Maiden's kisses (hard candies that resemble tiny satin pillows), peppermint straws, filled raspberries and peanuts, ribbon candy, and cut rock candy with flowers and designs blooming like cloisonné work — these are just a few of the sweets from the past. Most people also made candy for the

season, especially peanut brittle, divinity, and fudge. Making candy at home continued well into the postwar era, as the popularity of Mamie Eisenhower's fudge recipe proved when it was published in the early 1950s.

The postwar era also saw an explosion in new varieties of manufactured candy, and

IT WOULDN'T BE CHRISTMAS WITHOUT— *Whitman's* CHOCOLATES

Started in 1842

Whitman's Sampler

CHOCOLATES & CONFECTIONS

THE WORLD-FAMOUS SAMPLER
The best-known, best-liked box of candy—Christmas-wrapped. 1 lb. $2.00 2 lbs. $4.00

Whitman's CHOCOLATES

Merry Christmas *Whitman's* FAIRHILL CHOCOLATES ASSORTED SELECTED CENTERS

Antique Box

THE FAIRHILL
A choice selection—
Christmas-decorated. 1 lb. $1.50

THE ANTIQUE BOX
A fine assortment—
special Christmas label. 1 lb. $1.50

A WOMAN NEVER FORGETS THE MAN WHO REMEMBERS

these became part of the holiday tradition. Chocolates were especially popular, and just as people today might buy wine or flowers as a hostess gift, the offering of choice then was likely to be chocolates. Whitman established its Sampler as a must-have treat for families, but there were also boxes of chocolate-covered cherries, chocolate balls wrapped in foil to look like Christmas ornaments, and chocolate Santas. Numerous manufacturers made the most of the holiday season by coming up with special packaging, including Life Savers, which bundled an assortment of rolls together in a box that opened like a storybook.